THE
POWER
OF
MENTORSHIP
FOR THE HOME
BASED BUSINESS

www.The PowerOfMentorship.com
www.donboyer.org
www.DonBoyerAuthor.com

THE POWER OF MENTORSHIP
FOR THE HOME BASED BUSINESS
Published by Real Life Teaching/Publishing

donboyer@realifeteaching.com
www.DonBoyer.org
www.DonBoyerAuthor.com
562-789-1909
Whittier, California

Copyright © 2008 Real Life Teaching/Publishing
Library of Congress Control Number 2008920938
ISBN 978-1-60585-061-0

Cover Design by Mick Moore
www.KillerGraffix.com/www.QuickStartExpert.com

Editing, Composition, and Typography by Paulette Bethel
ProEditingService.com

Proofreading by The Pro Writing Co. www.ProWritingCo.com

This book is available at quantity discounts for bulk purchase.

For more information contact: Real Life Teaching/Publishing
donboyer@realifeteaching.com
Telephone: 562-789-1909
Whittier, California

Special Note: This edition of *The Power of Mentorship for the Home Based Business* is designed to provide information and motivation to our readers. It is sold with the understanding that the publisher is not engaged to render any type of psychological, legal, or any other kind of professional advice. The content of each article is the sole expression and opinion of its author, and not necessarily that of the publisher. No warranties or guarantees are expressed or implied by the publisher's choice to include any of the content in this volume. Neither the publisher nor the individual author(s) shall be liable for any physical, psychological, emotional, financial, or commercial damages, including but not limited to special, incidental, consequential or other damages. Our views and rights are the same: You are responsible for your own choices, actions, and results.

Printed in the United States of America

FIVE REASONS WHY I BELIEVE
THE POWER OF MENTORSHIP BOOK SERIES IS
THE MOST POWERFUL ON THE PLANET.

1. **Expanded Awareness.** The only way you will ever expand your finances, conditions, relationships and life is by expanding your awareness and consciousness in these areas. Bob Proctor once told me, "A person does not earn $100,000 a year because they want to, but because they do not have the awareness of how to earn $100,000 a month." If you want to expand your awareness you must listen to and surround yourself with those whose awareness is greater than yours. This is exactly what all the authors in this book series do for you.

Remember, who you listen to determines where you go, what you do and what you end up with...

2. **Treasure Map.** Finding treasure is a lot easier if you have a map from those who have already found it. Each chapter in *The Power of Mentorship* book series is like a treasure map to your dreams. If you follow the treasure map you will find your treasure in life.

3. **Thinking Bigger.** Our environment and conditions of our life are a direct reflection of our thinking. The problems in life are not based on lack or shortage of any kind but, rather, are based on small thinking. My earlier mentors taught me

that the only difference between a rich man and a poor man is their method of thinking. Each co-author will help you think bigger than you ever thought before.

4. **Hope.** Someone once said, "If you have hope in your future, you will have power in your today." From the highest mountain top to the lowest valley, these mentors inspire you to keep growing and going!

5. **Inspired Faith.** Albert Einstein said, "Only those who can see the invisible can do the impossible." Faith is the ability to see the invisible in order to grasp the incredible so that you can go out and do what the masses say is impossible. The *Power of Mentorship* books will help you build faith that you too can reach your dreams.

**Changing Lives
One Book At A Time**

FOREWORD

"THERE'S NO PLACE LIKE HOME"
Robin Jay

Home-based businesses are a $427 Billion dollar industry! Are you getting your share?

People are leaving corporate America in droves to work from home...consulting, selling, marketing, designing... experiencing and enjoying a life that is full of imagination and creativity. This new wave of home-based entrepreneurs was born from necessity and made possible by the Internet. Digital offices and virtual assistants have replaced hour-long commutes and the need for day care. Plus, people no longer have to settle for the emotional roller coaster of putting up with an obnoxious boss.

The birth and tremendous growth of home-based businesses was inevitable, as corporations began downsizing, commuters wasted time in traffic jams, and parents working outside the home were barely breaking even after paying for child care. The lure of working from home is irresistible to anyone who is fed up with life in the corporate fast lane.

But there are many unexpected pitfalls that can happen to anyone starting up or striving to succeed in a home-based business. Now you can take years off your learning curve by seeking the advice of mentors who have already launched businesses successfully. Whether you are struggling with a new business or you are launching a new home-based business from scratch, why not take advantage of the wisdom of these mentors? If you've been thinking about starting your own home-based business, or if your business is well under way, *The Power of Mentorship for the Home-Based Business* was written *just for you!*

Statistics show that a home-based business actually has a better chance of success than a traditional small business. According to the U.S. Small Business Administration's June, 2006 findings, there are more than 25 Million small businesses in the United States. But they are failing at an alarming rate. 2006 saw the start of 671,000 new businesses, while 544,800 businesses closed.

But 11 Million+ home-based businesses are thriving; helping Americans to enjoy a more peaceful and fulfilling lifestyle, instead of running themselves ragged on the corporate treadmill.

While the benefits to owning a home-based business are extraordinary, so are the opportunities to make mistakes. If you've never run your own business before, thinking you could run one now – without help – may be as foolish as trying to drive a car for the first time without a lesson. Maybe you have a tremendous amount of experience in a very small field. Maybe you know someone who pulls in a six-figure income selling products on eBay. And we all know entrepreneurs who are making huge incomes through network marketing. Whatever combination of experience or interest you have that is compelling you to pursue this new path, this one thing is certain: the more you know the better you'll do.

There are many unforeseen expenses and pitfalls; being armed and prepared will help you, the entrepreneur, to succeed more quickly. For instance, when you launch your business, you may not have a lot of expenses associated with it (as compared to opening a store, for instance). However, the fact that you will be running it out of your home makes the monthly expenses for your house a hard cost to running your business. It could take you a year or two before you realize where your business capital is going!

Inventory costs, if you have them, add up quickly, too. So do your regular business expenses. As a former advertising account manager, I saw many small businesses open their doors without any reserves left to advertise or market their business. If you are going to run a successful business, you have to tell people about it! Teddy Roosevelt once said that running a business without advertising is like winking at a pretty girl in the dark; only you know what you are doing!

Internet marketing can be more affordable than buying billboards or a radio campaign, but it's essential that you find a way to get the word out to the world about what you are doing.

Another advantage the internet has brought is that there are no borders to business anymore. You can sell products or services online to anyone – anywhere in the world. The potential is unlimited. So are the opportunities.

Arm yourself with the advice of those who have gone before you. I am fortunate enough to know many of the contributing authors to this book and can assure you that the information they share here will help you tremendously. I wish I had sought a mentor when I started my business. Now, I'm blessed to be surrounded by mentors every day. Surround yourself with them, too, and witness how quickly and easily you'll achieve the success you desire.

Best wishes for every success! ~ Robin Jay

ACKNOWLEDGMENTS

When you look at great accomplishments, what you are really seeing are the combined efforts, gifts, talents and skills of a magnificent team. There is no such thing as a lone ranger super star. You will find that there is no "I" in the word success, because success is always a by-product of "we." Everything that has been done in the Power of Mentorship community is the result of all our fantastic mentors.

Words can not express my gratitude for the following people who made this book a living reality:

My Lord, Jesus Christ
My wife and life partner, Melinda Boyer
My mentor, Bob Proctor
My wingman and partner, Mick Moore, and his wonderful wife, Manisha
Our editor, Paulette Bethel

All the co-authors and Mentors who contributed their knowledge to this book

Lisha and Kari Schneider
Bob Proctor
Amy Nowakowski
Brian Tracy
Sharon Hinckley
Gina Bell
Mick Moore
Lisa Jimenez

Paul and Sarah Edwards
Casey Emerson
George Ramirez
Kimberly Adams
DC Cordova
Dr. John Demartini
Marie Diamond
Paul Martinelli
Robin Jay
Shelley Kimberly
Vic Johnson
Dr. Tony Alessandra

All of you are my true heroes!

TABLE OF CONTENTS

INTRODUCTION

Don Boyer

There is a brand new group of people on the horizon who are taking the business world by storm; creating an abundance of wealth and making their mark in the world wide market place. Who are these people? The home based business professionals. They are the individuals who are leaving corporate America and coming home to purse their passion and dreams.

Government and industry reports show that increasing numbers of men and women are now opting to work out of their homes. In fact, the latest data from the U.S. Bureau of Labor Statistics shows that 4.12 million entrepreneurs are now working at home, most in a service based industry.

These are the ones who truly understand that wealth starts at home. Never before in the history of man has it been so easy for people to create financial independence and do business all around the globe — right from the comfort of their home. With the computers and internet technology we have today, working from home is no longer the lone road pitted with dangers and a high failure rate; it is now a proven model with a successful track record.

You do not need to look any further than your kitchen, bedroom, den, living room, or garage to find the foundation on which to build your business enterprise.

Following are four reasons why it pays to become the next home based business professional:

Introduction

1. **Personal Freedom:** The most exciting aspect of starting a home based business is the opportunity it provides to gain control over your own life. As a home business professional, you can shape your work life depending on your goals and desires. There are no bosses to follow, no corporate culture to abide by, and no rigid work schedules or time clocks. Instead, you have the freedom to work and earn as you choose, in the comfort of your own home. Of course, having all the time and freedom to work as you please also has its drawbacks. A home based professional needs to have good time management skills and discipline in order to push himself to work.

2. **Financial Rewards:** The financial benefits of working at home are very attractive. The convenience of having your office a few steps away from your bed allows you to save on commute time, gasoline, and transportation expenses. Since you work at home, you save on rental payments and overhead costs are cut significantly, allowing you to plow back all your capital and profits into the business. Your earning potential is directly proportional to your performance; no more waiting for your boss to give you your raise or promotion before you can increase your income. More importantly, however, a home business allows people who have been frequently shut out of the job market—homemakers, students, retirees, and the disabled, to name a few—to

create new income opportunities.

3. **Tax Advantages:** Using your home as a place of business offers a number of tax advantages. It allows you to deduct a part of the operating and depreciation expenses on your home. This means that a percentage of your rent or mortgage payment, depreciation, property taxes, insurance, utilities, and expenses for household maintenance, repairs, or improvements are deductible. You could also be entitled to deduct expenses from using a vehicle for your business, including gas, insurance, depreciation, and others. Consult your accountant for a careful evaluation of what can and cannot be deducted from using your home office. This is just more evidence that wealth does start at home.

4. **Passion:** As a home based entrepreneur, you are not boxed into one job and given a label identifying you as a secretary, banker, manager, or sales assistant. You are free to follow your passion and do the work that you love, work that brings you both profit and fulfillment while rendering a useful service or product to the market place. While it may mean a greater workload, the plus point is that you are doing work you enjoy and love and not doing work just for a pay-check. More importantly, you get to work and live based on your terms, not the terms of others.

IMAGINE waking up every day without worrying about getting ready for work, commuting to your dead end job, or answering to a boss... *ever again*!

In this powerful book you will find each mentor giving you insights, wisdom, ideas and techniques to help you take your home based business to the next level of success. Mentorship is the key factor to making any venture more successful and profitable. Learn from those who have accomplished that which you desire and you will find that you will reach your dreams and destination much faster with fewer struggles.

I encourage you to contact these mentors and let them help you reach your goals in every aspect of your life. They are here to help you say "Yes" to all of your dreams. Working from home is truly the business your boss hopes you never find out about! Here is to you, dear reader, for living life on your own terms!

Cheers!

Don Boyer

Lisha and Kari Schneider

Lisha and Kari are identical twins. They enjoy doubling their money and fun by working together. The twins began in the entertainment field by being stunt and body doubles for Mary-Kate and Ashley Olsen. After several movies and television parts, they were introduced to the travel business, becoming top female income earners in less than a year! In their first year they made over a six figure income which tripled the second year.

Lisha and Kari have been featured in national magazines as highly successful entertainers and business women entrepreneurs. They are authors of the book *Double Your Profits*, a step-by-step process on how to build a fast growing business in network marketing and become financially free. As Leisure Travel Consultants and

Lisha and Kari Schneider

Networking Specialists, they empower people to take Dream Vacations at wholesale prices and create the lifestyle they want to live.

They are one of the Mentors and wealth experts in *The Power of Mentorship* Movie with Bob Proctor and Marie Diamond from the Movie *The Secret*. They will empower you as you continue your exciting personal growth experience which can lead to financial freedom and a whole new lifestyle.

Telephone: (310) 466-8584
Email: Twins@TwinsTravelClub.com
Websites: www.TwinsTravelClub.com
www.TwinPower.biz

Chapter One

THE IDEAL HOME-BASED BUSINESS
Network Marketing
Lisha and Kari Schneider

There are three ways to make money:

You can work for a job
(J.O.B.) usually means "just over broke."
Most people do this just to pay their bills.

You can have money work for you.
This is a great way to make money if you have huge amounts of money to invest that will generate a monthly income – but most people don't have the large amount of seed money to start with.

You can have other people work for you.
This is network marketing. This is teaching people to do what you do to create a residual income. This way of making money is and has been used by the vast majority of wealthy people. Our country's first billionaire, Andrew Carnegie said, "I would rather earn one percent from the efforts of 100 people, than 100 percent from the efforts of myself."

Network marketing is a way to have other people work for you. Networking is like compounding pennies. If we gave you a choice of working for us for $1000 a day for a period of thirty-five days, versus working for yourself for one cent on the first day and doubling the amount each day for thirty-five days, which job offer would you take? Obviously, if you were to take the first choice, at the end of thirty-five days you would have $35,000. A wage of $35,000 in thirty-five days is phenomenal. Had you chosen the other alternative, you would be compounding your money at 100% per day.

1st day

$1000.....................$.01

15th day *(almost half way)*

$15,000....................$163.20

26th day

$26,000....................$331,500.00

35th day

$35,000....................$339,456,652.80

NOW – which choice do you favor?

Most people find it almost impossible to believe that one penny compounded at 100 percent per day is worth over a third of a billion dollars on the thirty-fifth day. The use of compounding is virtually the best way to make millions today!

FROM BEING IN DEBT
TO OVER A SIX-FIGURE INCOME
The First Year

After college we had one thing on our minds and that was to travel. We would work to save money for our next vacation, quit our jobs, travel until we were broke and start all over again. We then decided to pursue an acting career in Los Angeles but soon realized that in that profession, work wasn't steady. Bills came in faster than we could make money to pay them. We were deeply in debt when one of our good friends asked us if we liked to travel. As quickly as we told him that we loved to travel he showed us how to take five-star vacations at wholesale prices and get paid doing it.

We loved the idea of getting paid to travel and soon found most of our friends did, also. Within one year our debts were completely paid off and we were making more than a six-figure income, which tripled the next year.

We learned that in networking, you not only make money by your own efforts, you earn on the efforts of others. Another benefit of referral marketing which we continue to enjoy is passive reoccurring monthly income which allows us to be financially free.

FIVE STAR VACATIONS
AT WHOLESALE PRICES

The travel industry is booming because:

- More than 81 million older adults called Baby Boomers are planning to travel in the next year and will drive the market for the next 20 years.

- It is expected to double over the next decade.

- Travel is the single largest category of e-commerce, accounting for about 43% of all online spending.
  Dan Hess, May 6th 2005 CNN Money.

You can see it is the right opportunity at the right time!

One reason we are delighted to be involved in our specific

20

travel company is because of the technology that is now available. What used to take 3 hours, now takes about three minutes. The search engine technology searches dozens of websites simultaneously to get you the lowest possible prices on travel.

Another reason people are delighted to join our specific travel company is the Vacation Club for members only. Vacation packages include cruises from 4 to 14 days, safaris, golf-packages, all-inclusive international resorts, and sometimes include air fare. The prices seem unbelievable and are possible because of the company's buying power. It is similar to Sam's Club or Costco. We can buy in bulk and get the lowest rate because of our large membership base. Not only are these trips offered at prices everyone can afford, all the arrangements are made for you and you can take your family with you!

LIVING OUR DREAM
LIVING THE LIFESTYLE

Thanks to referral marketing, for the past several years we have been able to live the lifestyle we've always wanted. We set our own hours; we are our own bosses; we work from home with virtually no overhead; and best of all, we help others and get paid for it while constructing financial security for the rest of our lives with residual income.

When you are considering being in business with any networking company, you must consider three things: 1) the product 2) the business model or compensation plan 3) the training program. Our travel company exceeds all other travel companies in every one of these areas.

10 REASONS
We Decided to Own Our Own Business

1. **You can be your own boss.** Have you ever wanted to do things 'your way?' This is your chance. No wasted time, energy, or money. You decide the efficiency and success of the company as well as how fast your company will grow.

2. **You make your own schedule.** What are your best hours to work? Well, then those are your hours. You are free to fit your priorities into your work schedule, to enjoy your favorite hobbies, to spend time with your children and spouse according to their routines, and to vacation when you decide it's the best time.

3. **You choose the people with whom you wish to work.** Do you think you would be making more if it weren't for office politics? Have you even had a confrontation with your boss or fellow worker? Those things don't exist if you choose the people you work with.

4. **You work out of your own home.** Next time you find yourself in miserable traffic, think about the individuals, couples, families, retirees, students, previous heads of huge companies and professionals working from their comfortable living rooms, earning incredible incomes. There is absolutely nothing better than working from your home (or pool)!

5. **There is a low start-up cost. No high franchise fees.** No need to mortgage your house; no need to borrow money from a relative; no need to rob the kids' college

fund. A nominal startup fee (plus the tools to get started) just doesn't present a problem to anyone's budget. With an independent distributorship, rather than a franchise business, you do not continuously worry about the local government and insurance companies' attempts to control your business.

6. **You make money for yourself (and not just for your employer).** No matter how much faster a machinist works or how many more people an executive is in charge of, their salaries are not likely to change significantly. If *you* work harder and spend more hours on the job, *you* should benefit. People die of drop dead exhaustion while making a great profit for someone else. In networking, you benefit directly from your *own efforts.* And more spectacular than that, you benefit from *others efforts while they are benefiting themselves as well!* A real win-win!

7. **There are no limitations on your earnings.** You can contact as many people as you choose; you can build your organization and income as fast as you have hours in the day. There is no budget preventing overtime in your department. Just work and earn and grow! Your only limits are those you place on yourself!

8. **Major tax benefits for small business deductions.** Office supplies, auto expense & gas, phone, postage, publications, seminars, trainings, conventions, samples, fees, meeting supplies, awards, and gifts are just a few in a LONG list of deductions available for small business owners.

9. **Constructing financial security for the rest of your life with residual income. If you couldn't work, you still receive the income.** In networking, you are constructing an impermeable financial fortress around yourself and your family. What if you were injured in an accident or became sick? Recently a friend of ours went through a divorce and was unable to attend to her business. When her divorce was settled and she began actively doing the business again, she indicated to us that without the checks from her business, she would have never made it through. She also indicated that she could think of no other business where you could literally walk away and keep getting checks.

10. **You help others and get paid for it.** Networking is the truest form of this. In a regular job, you may or may not help others. In a regular job, it is always the boss who is paid the profits. In networking, the more you help others, the more you get. It feels good to get a monthly raise because you know that lives have been improved in direct relationship to that raise you received on your check. What a thrilling job. It is so easy to be passionate about something that can raise the quality of life for so many people on so many levels.

WE'LL MENTOR AND TRAIN YOU

It is the perfect time to join us in one of the fastest growing industries in the world and take control of your financial destiny. We have been able to help thousands change their own lives and the lives of their families. Call us now if you want to work a part or full time business from home, make millions in earnings, have a luxury home and an exotic car, travel to glamorous places, and have freedom to spend your days however you desire. We will personally train and mentor you to financial success. Take your first step now by watching www.TravelPresentation.com. To receive a free magazine featuring us in our home-based business and our company's success stories, contact us!

Bob Proctor

For 40 years, Bob Proctor has focused his entire agenda around helping people create lush lives of prosperity, rewarding relationships and spiritual awareness.

Bob Proctor knows how to help you because he comes from a life of want and limitation himself. In 1960, he was a high-school dropout with a resume of dead-end jobs and a future clouded in debt. One book was placed in his hands—Napoleon Hill's *Think and Grow Rich*—which planted the seed of hope in Bob's mind. In just months, and with further support from the works of Earl Nightingale, Bob's life literally spun on a dime. In a year, he was making more than $100,000 and soon topped the $1 million mark. It doesn't matter how you grew up, or what you've struggled with in life— your mind is unscathed by any circumstance you've struggled with in life—your mind is unscathed by any circumstance you've yet lived... and it's phenomenally powerful! Let Bob Proctor's live seminars, best-selling books and recordings show you how to excavate the wonderful gem of your own mind.

Visit Bob Proctor online at:
www.BobProctor.com

Chapter Two

IT BEGINS WITH YOUR DECISION
Bob Proctor

There is a single mental move you can make which, in a millisecond, will solve enormous problems for you. It has the potential to improve almost any personal or business situation you will ever encounter... and it could literally propel you down the path to incredible success. We have a name for this magic mental activity ... it is called DECISION.

Decisions or the lack of them are responsible for the breaking or making of many a career. Individuals who have become very proficient at making decisions, without being influenced by the opinions of others, are the same people whose annual incomes fall into the six and seven figure category. However, it's not just your income that is affected by decisions; your whole life is dominated by this power. The health of your mind and body, the well-being of your family, your social life, the type of relationships you develop ... all are dependent upon your ability to make sound decisions.

You would think anything as important as decision-making, when it has such far-reaching power would be taught in every school, but it is not. To compound the problem, not only is decision-making missing from the curriculum of our educational institutions, up until recently, it's also been absent from most of the corporate training and human resource programs available.

It Begins With Your Decision
Bob Proctor

So, how is a person expected to develop this mental ability? Quite simply, you must do it on your own. However, I think it's important to understand that it's not difficult to learn how to make wise decisions. Armed with the proper information and by subjecting yourself to certain disciplines, you can become a very effective decision maker.

You can virtually eliminate conflict and confusion in your life by becoming proficient at making decisions. Decision-making brings order to your mind, and of course, this order is then reflected in your objective world... your results. "It comes to pass. Environment is but our looking glass."

No one can see you making decisions but they will almost always see the results of your decisions. The person who fails to develop their ability to make decisions is doomed because indecision sets up internal conflicts which can, without warming, escalate into all out mental and emotional wars. Psychiatrists have a name to describe these internal wars, it is ambivalence. My Oxford Dictionary tells me that ambivalence is the co-existence in one person of opposite feelings toward the same objective.

You do not require a doctorate degree in psychiatry to understand that you are going to have difficulty in your life by permitting your mind to remain in an ambivalent state for any period of time. The person who does permit it to exist will become very despondent and virtually incapable of any type of productive activity. It is obvious that anyone who finds themselves in such a mental state is not living; at best, they are merely existing. A decision or a series of decisions would change everything.

A very basic law of the universe is "create or disintegrate." Indecision causes disintegration. How often have you heard a person say, "I don't know what to do." How often have you heard yourself say, "What should I do?" Think about some of the indecisive feelings you and virtually everyone on this planet experience from time to time.

LOVE THEM — LEAVE THEM

QUIT — STAY

DO IT — DON'T DO IT

GO BANKRUPT — NO DON'T

GO TO WORK — WATCH TV

BUY IT — DON'T BUY IT

SAY IT — DON'T SAY IT

TELL THEM — DON'T TELL THEM

Everyone, on occasion, has experienced these feelings of ambivalence. If it happens to you frequently, decide right now to stop it. The cause of ambivalence is indecision, but we must keep in mind that the truth is not always in the appearance of things.

Indecision is a cause of ambivalence, however it is a secondary cause, it is not the primary cause. I have been studying the behavior of people who have become very proficient at making decisions for over a quarter century. They all have one thing in common. They have a very strong self image, a high degree of self-esteem. They may be as different as night is to day in numerous other respects, but they certainly possess confidence.

30

It Begins With Your Decision
Bob Proctor

Low self-esteem or a lack of confidence is the real culprit here. Decision makers are not afraid of making an error. If and when they make an error in their decision, or fail at something, they have the ability to shrug it off. They learn from the experience but they will never submit to the failure.

Every decision maker was either fortunate enough to have been raised in an environment where decision making was a part of their upbringing, or they developed the ability themselves at a later date. They are aware of something that everyone, who hopes to live a full life, must understand: Decision making is something you cannot avoid.

That is the cardinal principle of decision making. DECIDE RIGHT WHERE YOU ARE WITH WHATEVER YOU'VE GOT. This is precisely why most people never master this important aspect of life. They permit their resources to dictate if and when a decision will or can be made. When John Kennedy asked Werner Von Braun what it would take to build a rocket that would carry a man to the moon and return him safely to earth, his answer was simple and direct. "The will to do it."

President Kennedy never asked questions, all of which would have, at that time, been valid. President Kennedy made a decision... he said, we will put a man on the moon and return him safely to earth before the end of the decade. The fact that it had never been done before in all the hundreds of thousands of years of human history was not even a consideration. He DECIDED where he was with what he had. The objective was accomplished in his mind the second he made the decision. It was only a matter of time —which is governed by natural law— before the goal was manifested in form for the whole world to see.

I was... just hours ago... in an office with three people. We were discussing the purchase of shares in a company. I was selling, they were buying. After a reasonable amount of time, one of the partners asked me when I wanted a decision. I replied, "Right now." I said, "You already know what you want to do."

There was some discussion about money. I pointed out that money had nothing to do with it. Once you make the decision you will find the money... every time. If that is the only benefit you receive from this particular message on decision-making, burn it into your mind. It will change your life. I explained to two of these people that I never let money enter my mind when I am deciding whether I will or will not do something. Whether I can afford it or not is never a consideration. Whether I want to or not is the only consideration. You can afford anything, there is an infinite supply of money. All of the money in the world is available to you, when the decision is firmly made. If you need money, you will attract it.

I am well aware there are any number of people who will say that is absurd. You can't just decide to do something if you do not have the necessary resources. And that's fine if that is the way they choose to think. I see that as a very limiting way of thinking. In truth, it probably is not thinking at all... it is very likely an opinion being expressed that was inherited from another older member of their family who did not think either.

It Begins With Your Decision
Bob Proctor

Do you give consideration to your thoughts? Do you consider how they affect the various aspects of your life? Although this should be one of our most serious considerations, for many people it is not. There are a very select few who make any attempt to control or govern their thoughts.

Anyone who has made a study of the great thinkers, the great decision makers, the achievers of history, will know they very rarely agreed on anything when it came to the study of human life. However, there was one point on which they were in complete and unanimous agreement and that was, "We become what we think about."

What do you think about? You and I must realize that our thoughts ultimately control every decision we make. You are the sum total of your thoughts. By taking charge this very minute, you can guarantee yourself a good day. Refuse to let unhappy, negative people or circumstances affect you.

The greatest stumbling block you will encounter when making important decisions in your life is circumstance. We let circumstance get us off the hook when we should be giving it everything we've got. More dreams are shattered and goals lost because of circumstance than any other single factor.

How often have you caught yourself saying, "I would like to do or have this but I can't because ..." Whatever follows "because" is the circumstance. Circumstances may cause a detour in your life but you should never permit them to stop you from making important decisions.

Napoleon said, "Circumstances; I make them." The next time you hear someone say they would like to vacation in Paris, or purchase a particular automobile but they can't because they don't have enough money, explain they don't need to worry about the money. Once the decision is made, they will figure out a way to get the amount needed. They always do.

Many misguided individuals try something once or twice and if they do not hit the bulls-eye, they feel they are a failure. Failing does not make anyone a failure, but quitting most certainly does and quitting is a decision. By following that form of reasoning, you would have to say when you make a decision to quit, you make a decision to fail.

Every day in America, you hear about a baseball player signing a contract which will pay him a few million dollars a year. You should try to keep in mind... that same player misses the ball more often than he hits it when he steps up to the plate. Everyone remembers Babe Ruth for the 714 home runs he hit and they rarely mention that he struck out 1,330 times.

Charles F. Kettering said, and I quote, "When you're inventing , if you flunk 999 times and succeed once, you're in."

That is true of just about any activity you can name, but the world will soon forget your failures in light of your achievements. Don't worry about failing, it will toughen you up and get you ready for your big win. Winning is a decision.

It Begins With Your Decision
Bob Proctor

Many years ago Helen Keller was asked if she thought there was anything worse than being blind. She quickly replied that there was something much worse. She said, "The most pathetic person in the world is a person who has their sight but no vision." I agree with Helen Keller.

At 91, J.C. Penney was asked how his eyesight was. He replied that his sight was failing but his vision had never been better. That is really great, isn't it?

Take the first step in predicting your own prosperous future. Build a mental picture of exactly how you would like to live. Make a firm decision to hold on to that vision and positive ways to improve everything will begin to flow into your mind.

Many people get a beautiful vision of how they would like to live but because they cannot see how they are going to make it all happen, they let the vision go. If they knew how they were going to get it or do it, they would have a plan not a vision. There is no inspiration in a plan but there sure is in a vision. When you get the vision, freeze frame it with a decision and don't worry about how you will do it or where the resources will come from. Charge your decision with enthusiasm... that is important. Refuse to worry about how it will happen.

Sometimes, it is advantageous to make decisions in advance: We make advanced bookings when we fly somewhere, that is quite common. We make advanced reservations to eliminate any confusion or problems when the time arrives for the journey. We do the same with renting a car, for the same reason. Think of the problems you will eliminate by making many of the decisions you must make well in advance.

I'll give you an excellent example. As I am preparing this message it is Ramadan, a time where all practising Muslims fast. I was in an office yesterday in Kuala Lumpur and was asked if I would like a cup of tea or coffee. I replied that I would appreciate a cup of tea. The lady next to me was then asked if she would like a cup and she replied ... "No, I'm fasting." When she was asked, she did not have to decide whether she wanted anything or not. Whether she was thirsty or not was not a tempered with discipline.

The exact same concept works with a person when they are on a diet to release weight. Their decisions are made in advance. If they are offered a big slice of chocolate cake, they don't have to say, "Gee, that looks good... I wonder if I should." The decision is made in advance.

I made a decision a long time ago that I would not participate in discussions of why something cannot be done. The only compensation you will ever receive for participating in or giving energy to that type of discussion, is something you do not want.

I always find it amazing at the number of seemingly intelligent people who persist in dragging you into these negative brainstorming sessions. In one breath these people tell you they seriously want to accomplish a particular objective. And, in the next breath, they begin talking about why they can't. Think of how much more of life they would enjoy by making a decision that they will no longer participate in that type of negative energy.

The humanistic psychologist, Dr. Abraham Maslow who devoted his life to studying self actualized people, stated very clearly that we should follow our inner guide and not be swayed by the opinion of others or outside circumstances. Maslow's research showed that the decision makers in life had a number of things in common; most importantly, they did work they felt was worthwhile and important. They found work a pleasure, and there was little distinction between work and play. Dr. Maslow said, to be self actualized you must not only be doing work you consider to be important, you must do it well and enjoy it.

Dr. Maslow recorded that these superior performers had values, those qualities in their personalities they considered to be worthwhile and important. Their values were not decisions. Like their work, they chose and developed their values themselves.

Your life is important and, at its best, life is short. You have the potential to do anything you choose, and to do it well. But, you must make decisions and when the time for a decision arrives, you must make your decision where you are with what you've got.

Let me leave you with the words of two great decision makers, William James and Thomas Edison. William James suggested that, compared to what we ought to be, we are making use of only a small part of our physical and mental resources. Stating this concept broadly, the human individual thus lives far within his limits. He possesses powers of various sorts which he habitually fails to use.

Years later, Thomas Edison said, and I quote, "If we all did the things we are capable of doing, we would literally astound ourselves."

By making a simple decision, the greatest minds of the past are available to you. You can literally learn how to turn your wildest dreams into reality.

Put this valuable information to use and recognize the greatness which exists within you. You have limitless resources of potential and ability waiting to be developed. Start today — there's never any time better than the present. Be all that you are capable of being.

Amy Nowakowski

Amy Nowakowski is a successful business manager with 22 years of technical engineering and program management experience in corporate aerospace, turned author, speaker, and consultant. An avid reader and constant student of success principles, Amy is an adjunct professor of business courses at the University of Phoenix and Kaplan University.

Amy's passion is to provide clients with valuable tools, tips, techniques, and consulting services to propel their business to achieve higher levels of success utilizing advanced communication skills, solid advice, and even a bit of humor.

Training is available on business planning and management topics that can be tailored to your organization to propel your work force to higher productivity and impeccable quality.

To contact Amy, visit her website:
www.InnovativeSolutionsGroup.us
or send an e-mail to amy@InnovativeSolutionsGroup.us
Phone: 877-679-7526

Chapter Three

BE *TOUGH*, BE SUCCESSFUL
Amy Nowakowski

Ching said, "It is only when we have the courage to face things exactly as they are, without any self-deception or illusion, that a light will develop out of events, by which the path to success may be recognized." When someone embarks on starting a home-based business, they often have grand ideas about how successful they will be, and are frequently disillusioned about what it takes to drive that very success. If, on the other hand, they start their business venture by taking a step back, putting a plan together, and then executing that plan with their eyes wide-open, success has a much higher probability of being realized. With a good plan in place, the missing link is execution to plan and good business management techniques. Putting a solid plan together and executing on that plan requires a unique set of leadership qualities that can drive success even in the most difficult circumstances. The following will provide guidance on the qualities of a successful leader, that when applied directly to business ventures and their business plans, will drive success.

Being TOUGH (Tenacious, Organized, Uncompromising on quality, Generous, and Hard working), when applied and driven throughout the organization, will lead to success. With these qualities built into the character of a leader, the organization will exude these values from every pore. Business owners can learn these qualities and teach them to their leadership team, instilling them into every employee. With these qualities always in the

41

forefront of every activity and decision, business owners will make better decisions that bring higher value to their customers. Home-based business owners can utilize and apply these values to their business even if they are the sole employee of their business, as these qualities apply to all businesses.

Be Tenacious

Starting a business is no feat for the faint of heart, or the easily swayed. Business owners expect setbacks, plan workarounds, enjoy peaks, weather valleys, and work very long days. The most successful business owners find a passion that burns deep within, that drives every molecule of their being to be tenacious in every act, driving success through the most difficult circumstances. Weathering each of these challenges requires persistence with a determination to resolve issues and a tenacity to succeed. Issues and challenges are met with a fierce and unrelenting determination to identify the root cause and brainstorm resolution options that can be evaluated with respect to risk association, and time to recovery. Only after exploring each alternative, and applying the best solution, will recovery be driven with the highest return and the least risk and cost.

Murphy's law states that if anything can go wrong, it will. The job of a business leader is to quickly regroup, restructure, and rebuild. The ability to analyze available viable options quickly and make decisions that have immediate impact takes tenacity and a strong will to win. Having the company vision clearly in mind will drive the choices made that, when implemented, will bring the company closer to achieving their vision. Not every action leads to success as planned, so being able to quickly regroup and change direction when necessary is critical to success in business.

Be Organized

Taking an organized approach to all activities daily will produce high value results that drive success throughout the organization. Every person has a method, or a system, they use for organizing their daily, weekly, monthly, and annual activities for peak productivity. Even having no system is a system. With computers in almost every home and business, it is difficult to imagine starting a business today without planning to utilize a computer. Purchasing the highest computing power possible within the available budget will provide the greatest payback and allow high productivity. Companies use computers as an organization tool utilizing many programs including project planning and managing software, word processors, internet access, e-mail capability, and any specialized software pertaining directly to the new business venture.

While computers are key to being organized, there are many times when computers are not available, and if not careful, business owners can become buried under the weight of paper notes everywhere without knowing the status of incidental critical actions associated with these activities. The types of activities in this category include managing the status of calls received and made, and actions taken and delegated. A simple method that has worked well for many years is to utilize a notebook that is small enough to carry around at all times and yet large enough to encompass at least a month's activities. Start at the beginning of the notebook and log each call received and made, with short notes about topics discussed, including any voice mail received. Then, turn to the back of the notebook and jot down each open action item that needs to be addressed. As the two ends of your notebook meet, you can review the month's accomplishments and transfer any open items to next month's notebook.

Creating a symbol key that is used for all actions in your notebook will help to know the status at a glance. An example of such a key is to precede each action with an open square. Add a dot to this open square when the action is started, and a check mark when the action is complete. In the event the activity was delegated to someone, or a voice message was sent that requires further follow up, notes can be added so that referring back to the action will quickly reveal the status of the action. An example of an action key is presented below. Create a key for your organization that is personalized, and can be used throughout for consistency and understanding by all employees.

☐ New/Not Started Activity

☑ Completed Activity

◼ Started Activity

◣ Message Left

△ Information

Using a hybrid between electronic and paper organizational tools works well in most circumstances.

44

The important thing is to have a system that works for your team, that is personalized, and that is utilized for all actions every day.

Be Uncompromising on Quality

Customers make purchases for their own reasons, and not necessarily for the reasons a business owner may think. Products and services must exude impeccable built in quality. Building quality into a product requires having repeatable processes and procedures utilized by every employee in the company throughout the development and production process. Each industry has a standard for measuring quality utilized by businesses and measured against industry criteria with resulting certifications. In some industries, companies are not invited to bid on projects if a certain quality level is not maintained.

Low quality products and services lead to increased cost to organizations to correct quality deficiencies, perform re-work, and improve or recover customer satisfaction. Building quality into products and services reduces these post-delivery costs and requires the efforts of every employee in an organization. Quality improvement initiatives are implemented to continually improve processes to reduce waste, evaluate performance, reduce process steps, and help employees be more efficient. Implementing these processes drives repeatability and thus higher quality. Customers are looking for the highest quality at the lowest cost, so driving high quality is critical to business success.

Be Generous

Customers want the most value for the least cost in a

product or service that requires minimal support, and that support is given freely and positively, if needed. Employees want the highest pay for an honest effort, where they feel appreciated and respected. This concept, when boiled down to the basic premise, leaves the idea of generosity where one always does the right thing in any situation with a happy spirit. If a customer was not happy with a product received for any reason, the right thing would be to offer an exchange, a full refund, or to compensate the customer for their inconvenience to their complete satisfaction.

Being generous in this way may seem like a huge expense as a business owner. Consider that an unhappy customer tells 10 or more people about their horrific experience, often relating why no one should ever deal with the offending business in the future. Then, consider that a happy customer may only tell one person what a great experience they had. Customers typically just go about their day without thinking about the great experience they just had. Once business owners begin to understand that doing the right thing and being generous with their clients and employees will provide a high future payback in repeat customers, more referrals, and less employee absenteeism, they will choose to be generous every time.

Generosity, like many other values in an organization, must start at the very top with the owner. The entire organization must drip generosity in every activity from every employee. This value of generosity, when taught and utilized in spirit, drives development of company processes and procedures for all company activities that provide highest value at the lowest cost. If a question arises, always err on the positive side for the other party, and give more than you receive.

Be Hard Working

Starting a business just may be the toughest thing you will ever do in your life. It may also be the most rewarding you ever embark on. As a business owner internalizes their vision, and becomes one with it, applying their passion in all activities, building the business may not even seem like work at all. Many business owners put in incredibly long hours for weeks on end, which may seem insane to the onlooker. To the business owner with a passion to build their dream business, the hours fly by like minutes on an egg timer.

Business owners must not only work hard, they must also work smart. Brian Tracy, master sales and leadership trainer, summed up working smart best when he said, "Don't do anything below your pay grade." What on earth, does he mean by this? Let me explain. Each individual brings a special value to an organization that is worth a specific amount of money to the company. If this individual brings a value of $150 per hour to the organization, then they would not be assigned to an activity that brings only $15 per hour of value. Utilizing each person's talent to their fullest potential allows the organization to work smart while working hard to accomplish activities that matter to business success.

A good plan, backed up by hard work that utilizes the Be TOUGH principle, will put your business on the road to success.

Brian Tracy

The following article was submitted by Brian Tracy, the most listened to audio author on personal and business success in the world today. He is the author/narrator of countless bestselling audio learning programs and the author of 16 books.

Contact Brian Tracy at:
Brian Tracy International
462 Stevens Ave., Suite 202
Solana Beach, CA 92075
Phone (858) 481-2977
www.BrianTracy.com

Chapter Four

LEADING AND MOTIVATING
Brian Tracy

It's been said that "Leadership is not what you do, but who you are." This, however, is only partially true. Leadership is very much who you are, but it cannot be divorced from what you do. Who you are represents the inner person, and what you do represents the outer person. Each is dependent on the other for maximum effectiveness.

The starting point of motivational leadership is to begin seeing yourself as a role model, seeing yourself as an example to others. See yourself as a person who sets the standards that others follow. A key characteristic of leaders is that they set high standards of accountability for themselves and for their behaviors. They assume that others are watching them and then setting their own standards by what they do. They, in fact, lead by example, just exactly as though someone were following them around, surreptitiously taking notes and photographs of their daily actions for others to see and act on.

Motivational leadership is based on the Law of Indirect Effort. According to this law, most things in human life are achieved more easily by indirect means than they are by direct means. You more easily become a leader to others by demonstrating that you have the qualities of leadership than you do by ordering others to follow your directions. Instead of trying to get people to emulate you, you concentrate on living a life that is so admirable that others want to be like you without your saying a word.

The Power of Mentorship For The Home Based Business
Don Boyer

In business, there are several kinds of power. Two of these are ascribed power and position power.

Position power is the power that comes with a job title or position in any organization. If you become a manager in a company, you automatically have certain powers and privileges that go along with your rank. You can order people about and make certain decisions. You can be a leader whether or not anyone likes you.

Ascribed power is the power you gain because of the kind of person you are. In every organization, there are people who are inordinately influential and looked up to by others, even though their positions may not be high up on the organizational chart. These are the men and women who are genuine leaders because of the quality of the people they have become, because of their characters and their personalities.

Perhaps the most powerful of motivational leaders is the person who practices what is called "servant leadership." Confucius said, "He who would be master must be servant of all." The person who sees himself or herself as a servant, and who does everything possible to help others to perform at their best, is practicing the highest form of servant leadership.

Over the years, we have been led to believe that leaders are those who stride boldly about, exude power and confidence, give orders and make decisions for others to carry out. However, that is old school. The leader of today is the one who asks questions, listens carefully, plans diligently and then builds consensus among all those who are necessary for achieving the goals. The leader does not try to do it by

50

himself or herself. The leader gets things done by helping others to do them.

This brings us to five of the qualities of motivational leaders. These are qualities that you already have to a certain degree and that you can develop further to stand out from the people around you in a very short period of time.

The first quality is *vision*. This is the one single quality that, more than anything, separates leaders from followers. Leaders have vision. Followers do not. Leaders have the ability to stand back and see the big picture. Followers are caught up in day-to-day activities. Leaders have developed the ability to fix their eyes on the horizon and see greater possibilities. Followers are those whose eyes are fixed on the ground in front of them and who are so busy that they seldom look at themselves and their activities in a larger context.

George Bernard Shaw summarized this quality of leaders in the words of one of his characters: "Most men look at what is and ask, 'Why?' I, instead, look at what could be and ask, 'Why not?'"

The best way for you to motivate others is to be motivated yourself.

The fastest way to get others excited about a project is to get excited yourself.

The way to get others committed to achieving a goal or a result is to be totally committed yourself.

The way to build loyalty to your organization, and to other people, is to be an example of loyalty in everything you say and do.

These all are applications of the Law of Indirect Effort. They very neatly tie in to the quality of vision.

One requirement of leadership is the ability to choose an area of excellence. Just as a good general chooses the terrain on which to do battle, an excellent leader chooses the area in which he and others are going to do an outstanding job. The commitment to excellence is one of the most powerful of all motivators. All leaders who change people and organizations are enthusiastic about achieving excellence in a particular area.

The most motivational vision you can have for yourself and others is to "Be the best!" Many people don't yet realize that excellent performance in serving other people is an absolute, basic essential for survival in the economy of the future. Many individuals and companies still adhere to the idea that as long as they are no worse than anyone else, they can remain in business. That is just plain silly! It is prehistoric thinking. We are now in the age of excellence. Customers assume that they will get excellent quality, and if they don't, they will go to your competitors so fast, people's heads will spin.

As a leader, your job is to be excellent at what you do, to be the best in your chosen field of endeavor. Your job is to have a vision of high standards in serving people. You not only exemplify excellence in your own behavior, but you also translate it to others so that they, too, become committed to this vision.

This is the key to servant leadership. It is the commitment to doing work of the highest quality in the service of other people, both inside and outside the organization. Leadership today requires an equal focus on the people who must do the job, on the one hand, and the people who are expected to benefit from the job, on the other.

The second quality, which is perhaps the single most respected quality of leaders, is *integrity*. Integrity is complete, unflinching honesty with regard to everything that you say and do. Integrity underlies all the other qualities. Your measure of integrity is determined by how honest you are in the critical areas of your life.

Integrity means this: When someone asks you at the end of the day, "Did you do your very best?" you can look him in the eye and say, "Yes!" Integrity means this: When someone asks you if you could have done it better, you can honestly say, "No, I did everything I possibly could."

Integrity means that you, as a leader, admit your shortcomings. It means that you work to develop your strengths and compensate for your weaknesses. Integrity means that you tell the truth, and that you live the truth in everything that you do and in all your relationships. Integrity means that you deal straightforwardly with people and situations and that you do not compromise what you believe to be true.

If the first two qualities of motivational leadership are vision and integrity, the third quality is the one that backs them both up. It is *courage*. It is the chief distinguishing characteristic of the true leader. It is almost always visible in the leader's words and actions. It is absolutely indispensable to success, happiness and the ability to motivate other people to be the best they can be.

In a way, it is easy to develop a big vision for yourself and for the person you want to be. It is easy to commit yourself to living with complete integrity. But it requires incredible courage to follow through on your vision and on your commitments. You see, as soon as you set a high goal or standard for yourself, you will run into all kinds of difficulties and setbacks. You will be surrounded by temptations to compromise your values and your vision. You will feel an almost irresistible urge to "get along by going along." Your desire to earn the respect and cooperation of others can easily lead to the abandonment of your principles, and here is where courage comes in.

Courage combined with integrity is the foundation of character. The first form of courage is your ability to stick to your principles, to stand for what you believe in and to refuse to budge unless you feel right about the alternative. Courage is also the ability to step out in faith, to launch out into the unknown and then to face the inevitable doubt and uncertainty that accompany every new venture.

Most people are seduced by the lure of the comfort zone. This can be likened to going out of a warm house on a cold, windy morning. The average person, when he feels the storm swirling outside his comfort zone, rushes back inside where it's nice and warm. But not the true leader. The true leader has the courage to step away from the familiar and comfortable and to face the unknown with no guarantees of success. It is this ability to "boldly go where no man has gone before" that distinguishes you as a leader from the average person. This is the example that you must set if you are to rise above the average. It is this example that inspires and motivates other people to rise above their previous levels of accomplishment as well.

Alexander the Great, the king of Macedonia, was one of the most superb leaders of all time. He became king at the age of 19, when his father, Philip II, was assassinated. In the next 11 years, he conquered much of the known world, leading his armies against numerically superior forces.

Yet, when he was at the height of his power, the master of the known world, the greatest ruler in history to that date, he would still draw his sword at the beginning of a battle and lead his men forward into the conflict. He insisted on leading by example. Alexander felt that he could not ask his men to risk their lives unless he was willing to demonstrate by his actions that he had complete confidence in the outcome. The sight of Alexander charging forward so excited and motivated his soldiers that no force on earth could stand before them.

The fourth quality of motivational leadership is *realism*. Realism is a form of intellectual honesty. The realist insists upon seeing the world as it really is, not as he wishes it were. This objectivity, this refusal to engage in self-delusion, is a mark of the true leader.

Those who exhibit the quality of realism do not trust to luck, hope for miracles, pray for exceptions to basic business principles, expect rewards without working or hope that problems will go away by themselves. These all are examples of self-delusion, of living in a fantasyland.

The motivational leader insists on seeing things exactly as they are and encourages others to look at life the same way. As a motivational leader, you get the facts, whatever they are. You deal with people honestly and tell them exactly what you perceive to be the truth. This doesn't mean that you will always be right, but you will always be expressing the truth in the best way you know how.

The fifth quality of motivational leadership is *responsibility*. This is perhaps the hardest of all to develop. The acceptance of responsibility means that, as Harry Truman said, "The buck stops here."

The game of life is very competitive. Sometimes, great success and great failure are separated by a very small distance. In watching the play-offs in basketball, baseball and football, we see that the winner can be decided by a single point, and that single point can rest on a single action, or inaction, on the part of a single team member at a critical part of the game.

Life is very much like competitive sports. Very small things that you do, or don't do, can either give you the edge that leads to victory or take away your edge at the critical moment. This principle is especially true with regard to accepting responsibility for yourself and for everything that happens to you.

The opposite of accepting responsibility is making excuses, blaming others and becoming upset, angry and resentful toward people for what they have done to you or not done for you.

Any one of these three behaviors can trip you up and be enough to cost you the game:

> If you run into an obstacle or setback and you make excuses rather than accept responsibility, it's a five-yard penalty. It can cost you a first down. It can cost

you a touchdown. It can make the difference between success and failure.

If, when you face a problem or setback, and you both make excuses and blame someone else, you get a 10-yard penalty. In a tightly contested game, where the teams are just about even, a 10-yard penalty can cost you the game.

If, instead of accepting responsibility when things go wrong, you make excuses, blame someone else and simultaneously become angry and resentful and blow up, you get a 15-yard penalty. This may cost you the championship and your career, as well, if it continues.

Personal leadership and motivational leadership are very much the same. To lead others, you must first lead yourself. To be an example or a role model for others, you must first become an excellent person yourself.

You motivate yourself with a big vision, and as you move progressively toward its realization, you motivate and enthuse others to work with you to fulfill that vision.

You exhibit absolute honesty and integrity with everyone in everything you do. You are the kind of person others admire and respect and want to be like. You set a standard that others aspire to. You live in truth with yourself and others so that they feel confident giving you their support and their commitment.

You demonstrate courage in everything you do by facing doubts and uncertainties and moving forward regardless. You put up a good front even when you feel anxious about the outcome. You don't burden others with your fears and misgivings. You keep them to yourself. You constantly push yourself out of your comfort zone and in the direction of your goals. And no matter how bleak the situation might appear, you keep on keeping on with a smile.

You are intensely realistic. You refuse to engage in mental games or self-delusion. You encourage others to be realistic and objective about their situations as well. You encourage them to realize and appreciate that there is a price to pay for everything they want. They have weaknesses that they will have to overcome, and they have standards that they will have to meet, if they want to survive and thrive in a competitive market.

You accept complete responsibility for results. You refuse to make excuses or blame others or hold grudges against people who you feel may have wronged you. You say, "If it's to be, it's up to me." You repeat over and over the words, "I am responsible. I am responsible. I am responsible."

Finally, you take action. You know that all mental preparation and character building is merely a prelude to action. It's not what you say but what you do that counts. The mark of the true leader is that he or she leads the action. He or she is willing to go first. He or she sets the example and acts as the role model. He or she does what he or she expects others to do.

You become a motivational leader by motivating yourself. And you motivate yourself by striving toward excellence, by committing yourself to becoming everything you are capable of becoming. You motivate yourself by throwing your whole heart into doing your job in an excellent fashion.

Leading and Motivating
Brian Tracy

You motivate yourself and others by continually looking for ways to help others to improve their lives and achieve their goals. You become a motivational leader by becoming the kind of person others want to get behind and support in every way.

Your main job is to take complete control of your personal evolution and become a leader in every area of your life. You could ask for nothing more, and you should settle for nothing less.

This article was submitted by Brian Tracy, the most listened to audio author on personal and business success in the world today. He is the author/narrator of countless best-selling audio learning programs and the author of 16 books. All rights reserved worldwide. Copyright © 2006.

Sharon Hinckley, Watercolorist

Sharon Hinckley's paintings are a reflection of the Light that she sees in our world.

Originally from Chevy Chase, Maryland, Sharon Hinckley is a graduate of Stanford University. She has traveled the world painting and teaching on locations wherever she goes. In the manner of the Impressionists and "Plein Air" painters, she works from life. She now lives in La Jolla, California with her husband and a "fur person."

For the past eight years she has been a featured Artist with the La Jolla Historical Society's Secret Garden Tour. She has had numerous one-woman shows and her work is represented in many private and corporate collections including Bank of America, and the Taipei National Museum of History.

She is the author of NorthLight Books' *Watercolor Basics Painting Flowers*, and a contributor to *The Big Fat Book of Watercolor Basics*. In 2004, she won the First Prize Award at the Keyes Gallery "Plein Air" Painting Competition.

In addition to her love of art, Sharon loves the inner art of Yoga. Not only does she enjoy her own practice, she is a registered and certified Hatha Yoga teacher as well as a Dahn Instructor.

Sharon welcomes students of all levels to her classes and tours. And, of course, commissions are cheerfully accepted!

"In the photo, I am wearing a hat that I designed myself."

Visit Sharon Hinckley online at:
www.SharonHinckley.com

Chapter Five

PUTTING YOUR HEART INTO ART
Sharon Hinckley

Our thoughts are truly more powerful than we can ever possibly imagine. In April of 2005, I became associated with a rapidly growing Spiritual group. Last year, I asked a long time member if she would be my Mentor. She is an incredibly busy woman and yet she told me, "Sharon, I always have time for you." What a powerful boost this has been for my psyche to have someone who #1—always has time for me, and #2—is willing to let me know where I am coming up short and help me make the correction. While Nancy is my first "official" mentor, there have been many who have served me in that role whether or not they had an official title.

I am a professional artist. Since 1975, I have been selling my Plein-Air Watercolor Paintings as well as teaching classes and workshops, serving as the mentor to a new group of aspiring artists.

I came into the world on a fortuitous day: January 12! Historically, this has been a good day for artists to arrive on earth. On this day were born Thomas Moran, John Singer Sargeant, Juiseppe Ribera, and Sharon Smull. The name "Hinckley" came later. I have heard that it is important to choose your parents carefully. Unfortunately, my parents weren't connoisseurs of Fine Art, at least not my early work!

According to my recollection, my "career" started around the age of four. I remember making a very large mural in crayon on the living room wall. Unfortunately, the "P's" were not impressed with either my design or the placement of color and I was sent to bed without any supper! Since that unfortunate incident, most of the critics have been kinder!

Lesson #1 Be willing to persist even in the face of poor reviews.

In any case, I kept drawing. I especially loved to draw horses and cats and animals and flowers and trees. Eventually, I started getting some encouragement on the homefront. My grandfather gave me the book *How to Draw* by Victor Perard. It cost $3.75. It was filled with pictures of cats, dogs, horses, people, trees and buildings. I both traced these images and copied them over and over and over again! I had *Drawing Animals* also by Perard and *How to Draw Horses* by Walter Foster. I drew and I drew and I drew.

Lesson #2 Practice, Practice, Practice

When I was 10 years old my dad bought a boat. So I added sailboats and water scenes to my sketchbooks. About this time, my dad gave me a small palette made by the Grumbacher paint company. This palette is made of white plastic and has 19 wells for color. The palette came with tubes of student grade watercolor paints. This was one of my first forays into the field of watercolor. I wasn't very happy with either the paint or my early watercolor paintings. However, I love that palette. In fact, it is the best palette I have ever found. More than 50 years later, I am still using the palette that my dad gave me when I was a little girl.

Lesson #3 Be grateful for your benefactors even when you can't make use of all their gifts. Express that gratitude frequently, loudly and in person!

As a child I was not very coordinated. I was not good at competitive sports. My gross motor coordination was poor, and my fine motor coordination was pretty gross too! I was so frustrated. I simply didn't have the physical ability—yet—to do what I wanted to do. I was sure that I didn't have the "talent" to ever be an artist.

Lesson #4 Realize that you will have periods of doubt and frustration. Indeed, "losing the way" may actually be part of "the way."

Despite apparent lack of skill and talent, I kept drawing. If nothing else, I am definitely stubborn! I was blessed to have attended the Sidwell Friends School in Washington DC. While art lessons were offered in the lower grades, at that time there were no art classes given to the Upper School students. However, the Friends School made special arrangements so that I could continue to have art classes during all four years of High School. This was not something that I requested. The School took it upon itself to see that I received this training. Russell and Betty Hoagland were the art teachers who truly encouraged and nurtured my budding talent all the while, literally, trying to help me put things into proper perspective!

Lesson #5 There are people who will see your gifts even when you can't. Be willing to hear what they have to say.

In the Fall of 1963, I entered Stanford University. At that time, I thought that I wanted to study "Spanish" or

64

"Psychology." After my freshman year, I don't believe I ever took another class in either one of those subjects. I was interested in the "nuts and bolts" of painting, not the theory. Stanford offered a lot of theory but not very many nuts or bolts! I did take a few studio art classes, but for the most part, they didn't suit my interests so I decided to major in Art History. I thought it would give me a good background if I ever decided to actually paint—which I was sure I would never have the courage to do.

Lesson #6 You will go through fallow periods where you do not appear to be progressing, yet you may be gaining valuable experience!

I graduated from college on June 18. I waited all of 24 hours before getting married on June 19. The next five years remain sort of a blur. We moved every few months, my husband held several jobs, then entered Military service. I was a department manager for a trendy Department Store, did volunteer work in hospitals, traveled to Bermuda with my grandmother, bought handbags for another large store, had a baby, and moved again. As I recall my "Artwork" during these years consisted of painting walls and hanging wallpaper!

Eventually, I settled in Los Altos, California in a small house with my husband, baby, and a part time job as the bookkeeper for The Adventure Travel Agency. When I was working for the travel agency a very accomplished artist named Jane Burnham came to promote a painting trip that she was leading to Mexico.

Jane's work has won many awards, her trips are popular and her paintings are beautiful! However, on this particular day, her painting demonstration was NOT going well. She was painting a market scene only it just wasn't working. Everything that she did—more chickens, more donkeys, more sombreros—to improve the painting just made it worse and worse and worse. That painting was a dog!

I didn't take the trip to Mexico, but I made a huge discovery that day. If an artist as talented and accomplished as Jane Burnham* could make a painting that was not successful maybe there was hope even for me!!

Lesson #7 It is OK to make a mistake. Jane taught me this beautiful saying by Thoreau, "If the only birds that sang were the birds that sang the best, the woods would be silent."

It was here that I found my courage. I quit my job and decided to take courses at Foothill, the local community college. In those days, I thought I was supposed to paint in oil. To start, I signed up for two classes: one in oil painting and one in design. My son was very excited for me as well as he thought I had said I was going to go to "Football College." It doesn't get much better than that, right? Wrong!

My first day of class was a disaster; I couldn't stand either class. Help! What was I going to do??? I had quit my job and, if I didn't go to "Football College," I was going to disgrace myself in front of my family. I dropped the classes that I signed up for, and tried to find some sort of replacement. I ended up signing up for a course in "Layout" which is now known as "graphic design," and a watercolor class taught by Brian dePalma. Why I chose watercolor I don't know as my prior experiences with watercolor paint had been anything but happy. After all, watercolor is runny, messy, and impossible to control! Besides, "all serious Art is done in oil."

I shall never forget the first painting that I made in dePalma's class. He told us to go out and paint a dark shape against a light shape. I did. I painted a light green leaf against a dark background, and I won the "prize" that day for making the painting with the most contrast. Ever since that day, that is basically what I have been doing: painting Light Shapes against Dark Shapes. I threw that painting away. Actually, I threw away 600 more paintings before I made one that I thought was worth keeping. But I did keep painting.

Lesson #8 (see Lesson #2 – Practice, Practice, Practice)

I went on to take some classes at San Jose State University studying with some professors who had, in fact, taught at Stanford shortly before I matriculated there.

Lesson #9 If you miss the brass ring the first time around you *can* have another chance.

At San Jose State, I studied Graphic Design with Raymond Brose. I even took some industrial design courses. At last, I was getting my nuts and bolts! Dr. Brose helped me not only with my technique; he actually showed me how to be more at ease with my work.

I also discovered painting workshops. I began taking workshops from Professional Artists who earned their living from their paintings. I studied with Rex Brandt, Millard Sheets, Bob Landry, George Post, Tom Nash, Dorner Shuler, and Zoltan Szabo. While none of these people were "official mentors" I was learning from every single one of them. One of my greatest honors is to have my work included in the *Big Fat Book of Watercolor Basics* which is dedicated to my teacher Zoltan Szabo.

Lesson #10 It is important to get the training that you need no matter where you have to go to find it!

At "Football College" I met a fellow student named Kim Manfredi. Kim both painted and made pottery. As I tend to go off it all directions at the same time, for once, I wisely set a limit and decided that I would focus on watercolor painting alone. Kim and I regularly went out to paint in the Santa Clara Valley. I joined the Santa Clara Valley Watercolor Society becoming their "Noble Leader" in 1977. For several years, Kim served as my primary critic and, of course, the other members of the Watercolor Society gave me a great deal of support as well. Kim, the members of the Watercolor Society, and the workshop instructors all served to mentor and guide me. My main mentor, however, has always been the Earth herself. Constantly going back to nature has both refreshed and guided me with each painting teaching me enough to do the next one.

In December of 1975, Kim and I had our first exhibition. We called it *"The Holiday Studio Show"* and it was held in our Los Altos living room. We invited friends and neighbors and anyone we could think of. Kim sold her pots and I sold my paintings. It was a big enough success that we did it again and again and again.

Lesson #12 The best way to get started is to start!

In October of 1978, my husband, young son and I left

68

Putting Your Heart Into Art
Sharon Hinckley

California to live in Asia for what turned out to be five years. Our first assignment was to Taiwan. We arrived just in time for the United States to normalize relations with China and our shipment, containing my precious paints, got lost on the way to Taipei. Eventually, our shipment was located and I was able to get my art supplies. At that time, it was illegal to paint out of doors on Taiwan. Being somewhat of a brat, I did it anyway. Since I had survived the P's sending me to bed without my supper, I figured that I could survive the local authorities as well! And I did. I continued with my painting—even teaching some art classes. I had numerous exhibitions in Taiwan at local business clubs, The Taipei American Club, and the National Museum of History.

While living in Asia, I made frequent trips to the United States. My dad gave me huge support arranging Exhibitions for me at the University Club in Washington DC and framing my artwork as well. I also had a one-woman show at the Rosicrucian Museum in San Jose, California.

After living on Taiwan for three years we moved to Tokyo where I continued to paint and to exhibit. Again, I showed my work at clubs including the Taipei American Club. My last exhibit in Japan was held at Kato's Gallery.

In 1984, I moved to La Jolla, California where I am still living with my husband and a "fur person." Since we have been here, I have continued painting, learning and teaching. I have served as the president of The Artists Guild and as a Board Member of the San Diego Museum of Art. In 1999, I became a registered and certified Hatha

Yoga instructor. I joined the faculty of the Athenaeum Art School in La Jolla.

In 2004, in addition to the Plein Air Paintings, I have also begun making Play-in-Air (abstract) acrylic paintings. In 2005, I also became a Dahn instructor. I have added giclee reproductions of my artwork to my repertoire. In May of 2007, I started a greeting card company, selling 300 cards the first week I was in business. I am not exactly sure how to create a greeting card business. In fact, in the age of the computer, it almost seems counter intuitive to start a greeting card line. Yet many shops say that greeting cards are their #1 sellers. So far, I have my work in 19 shops. Most of all, I am having fun making the cards and meeting the people. **The best way to get started is to start!**

Lesson #13 "It is never too late to be what you might have been." George Elliot.

*Years later, I called Jane. I told her this story and that this experience was what had given me the courage to begin my own Art career. I told her that while I would continue to tell the story, I would never reveal her name without her permission. Being the gracious soul that she is, Jane said that she would be delighted to have me use her name!

Gina Bell

Gina Bell is a Daring Divapreneur who enjoys working with self-employed women who find themselves stuck in business or life and don't know why.

Gina's fun, kick-in-the-pants approach to success planning, marketing and mentorship empowers women to be more daring; to reach beyond where they are to where they want to be.

Go to www.daringdivapreneur.com now for valuable tips and advice. Be sure to claim your FREE eBook entitled *Oh Yes There Is a Daring Divapreneur in YOU!* with gift subscription to Gina's business boosting eZine!

Chapter Six

NOT SURE YOU CAN SUCCEED?
Get a Believability Makeover!
Gina Bell

I used to believe that success involved setting a series of goals and then doing what was necessary to achieve them. Set the goals, determine the actions and get it done. It seemed like a perfectly logical plan but I soon realized that when it comes to success, perfectly logical plans sometimes don't work.

Setting goals and not achieving them became awfully frustrating very fast. It was a puzzle to me and I started to doubt that I would ever be the success that I dreamed of being. Were my goals set too high? Was I doing the wrong things? What could I do differently?

I became highly determined to solve the mystery of my unachieved successes and at some level I knew that I wasn't going to be able to do it alone. A mentor helped me to discover that sometimes we *think* we're doing the right things when in reality our internal beliefs aren't aligned with what we *really* want. And sometimes we know exactly what we must do to accomplish a goal but limiting beliefs keep us from actually doing it.

Once I realized what was going on it made perfect sense. I wasn't getting the results I wanted because my beliefs dictated my habits which dictated my results. My beliefs influenced my decisions which sabotaged my goals. Did you know success is first an inside job? But what does that really mean?

I learned that self-belief is one of the greatest gifts we can give ourselves and is absolutely essential for success. Belief is the fire that fuels our vision; allows us to dream and paves the way for accomplishments and rewards.

The opposite of belief is distrust. When we don't trust ourselves we hesitate and even get completely stuck! If you expect to fail, in most cases you already have. On the other hand, if you believe without a shadow of a doubt that you will succeed, then it will become your reality.

Now that I was aware that limiting beliefs were preventing me from reaching my goals, I needed to find out how to change it so that I could be more successful. What DID I believe? Why were my beliefs sabotaging my success? How could I build my believability and confidence so that I could become more successful?

Are there certain things that you believe you CAN'T achieve? What beliefs do you have that are keeping you from achieving your goals? Perhaps, you aren't sure your business will succeed. Maybe you believe that if you make too much money it will change you in a negative way or change your life in a way that scares you? Maybe you don't believe that you deserve to be successful?

The great thing about belief is that you can choose what to believe. How would you like to eliminate negative beliefs that are holding you back and replace them with positive, supportive beliefs that build you up for success? If your answer is yes read on, dear friends, as I'll be getting to the "how" in just a moment.

Our belief systems are programmed over time, beginning in childhood. Our parents, grandparents, teachers, siblings and other adult role models told us we were too little or too young or not smart enough to do certain things and as adults, small failures at school and at work reinforce a sense of inability.

The beliefs we hold now as adults instigate our emotions and behaviours. When the beliefs are limiting in nature this becomes a barrier to positive decision making and action. For example, if you unknowingly hold the belief that "To be successful you need a college degree," your decisions, emotions and behaviours will reflect this belief. Making decisions that moves you closer to success when you don't have a college degree will be difficult and you'd likely be blind to many opportunities that come along. In your mind, you're a failure until/unless you have the degree. The important thing to remember is that your beliefs create your reality. Is this a reality you want?

Let me give you some examples of some other common limiting beliefs. Some of them may sound familiar to you:

"Money doesn't grow on trees!"
"No pain, no gain."
"You can't have your cake and eat it too"

74

Not Sure You Can Succeed? Get a Believability Makeover!
Gina Bell

"Money can't buy happiness"
"I can do it myself"
"This time of year is always slow"
"If I didn't have bad luck I wouldn't have any luck at all"

Beliefs can sometimes seem to be more truth, or fact, rather than a choice we are making yet, in reality, we are always subconsciously reviewing and choosing our beliefs. Our beliefs have evolved and will continue to change throughout our lives. Did you believe in Santa Claus or The Tooth Fairy when you were a child? Its likely those beliefs have changed. And don't forget, people used to believe the Earth was flat proving that sometimes we just don't know any better. And that's okay because beliefs adjust as we learn and experience new things; i.e., today we know the Earth is round.

So, if our beliefs are constantly changing and we aren't even aware that it is happening, what would come about if we did become aware of the changes? What if we started to consciously choose and accept beliefs that support the feelings and behaviours we want to have and create the life we really want for ourselves?

Once we realize that we can take control of our own beliefs, the seemingly impossible really does start to become the possible. Today, many of the things I was convinced were impossible for me can be found on my list of accomplished goals and they can be for you, too!

Before you read any further find a pen and some paper.

At the top of the first sheet title the page "What Success Means to Me." On the second sheet of paper, create two columns, one titled "My Now Beliefs" and the other column titled "My NEW Beliefs." Now let's begin the process of transforming your beliefs to get you from where you are now to where you really want to be!

5-Step Believability Makeover:

Step 1: Get Your "Inner Voice" Talking

To identify your limiting beliefs you need to get your inner voice talking. I've found the most effective method is through writing and journaling. To uncover the beliefs that are holding you back from success, begin defining what success means to you. What are your goals? Who do you really want to be? What will you do? How will you act? This will provide the contrast and dialogue needed to get your inner voice talking!

Write down everything that comes to mind. Be as specific and descriptive as possible from the clothes you will wear to the cars you will drive and the charities you will give to. As you write, your inner voice will start speaking to you. It's important to do this in a quiet place so that you can pay close attention to how your mind is responding.

Step 2: Identify and List Your Limiting Beliefs

Now that a dialogue is starting to unfold, continue to work on your definition of success and begin to list any limiting beliefs that arise in the process. Write down the negative or self-defeating thoughts that pop into your mind. Some of your limiting beliefs will be obvious and you'll know exactly where they come from while others will be more elusive and require digging deeper. This is where a coach, mentor or trusted colleague can help you to brainstorm and look back at past choices to identify any limiting beliefs that aren't as obvious.

Here's an example: If your dream is to drive a Lexus but your inner voice says "only wannabes drive a Lexus" you have just identified a limiting belief to that specific goal. The more specific you are, the easier it will be for you to uncover your limiting beliefs.

Step 3: Choose new beliefs that support your dreams
By questioning the truth of each limiting belief and defining how the belief has been holding you back you create an opportunity to change it. For each of your limiting beliefs, think about how the belief holds you back and decide how you want to be, act or feel in its place.

For example, I used to believe that "I can't afford to hire a bookkeeper." This belief was holding me back because it required that I invest my valuable time doing something I'm not trained or skilled at doing (and don't enjoy doing, at all)! I never really knew if I was doing it right either... who knows how much income tax I could have saved? (By the way, this particular belief also revealed other limiting beliefs that I had about money and my ability to be successful!) I could not prove it to be an absolute truth and it did not support my vision of success so I decided to change it. It made more sense to focus my time on revenue generating activities and in doing so this would create the opportunities and revenue that I needed to hire a bookkeeper. I could stop worrying about errors, too, because I would hire a trained expert, etc...

Step 4: Strengthen Your Believability with Affirmation Statements

Now that you have chosen new beliefs that are positive and support your dreams, you need to re-program your inner voice to be aligned with where you want to be. Title a third sheet of paper "My Affirmation Statements."

Your next step is to create and write down an empowering affirmation statement for each new belief.

Affirmations give you permission to be the successful and accomplished person you dream of being. My affirmation statement from the above example might be: "My time is valuable. Hiring an expert allows me to stay focused on revenue generating activities and I can relax knowing my bookkeeping is done right."

Read your affirmation statements several times a day and say them out loud to reinforce your new beliefs. Future decisions and behaviours will stem from a belief system that supports your path to success and happiness.

Step 5: Have Faith

Your believability makeover is almost complete and it's important to keep in mind that overwriting some of your past beliefs will take time and persistence. Sometimes the transformation doesn't happen as quickly as we'd like but that doesn't mean it's not going to work. Just remember, your old beliefs were sabotaging your success. You're in the driver's seat now.

As you grow and learn, you'll likely uncover other limiting beliefs. Keep working at it - after all, it's your success that's on the line. Having faith removes resistance and allows good to flow to you. Trust in the process, have faith in your ability to achieve your goals and never give up.

There are other things you can do too! First, surround yourself with people who already believe in you. Sometimes their belief can be enough to keep you motivated and to pick you up when you fall, until such time as your belief is enough on its own. I was fortunate to have a doting Father who believed that I could do anything. I know it's kind of a father- daughter thing but it always meant the world to me. Many times, his belief in me was enough to keep me going. Just the thought of disappointing him was motivation enough. Even though he's gone, I am forever stronger because of his belief in me. It allowed me to see opportunity and success that could be mine through his eyes.

If you find it difficult to overcome certain beliefs hire a mentor or coach to guide you through the process. You may be too close to the issue to see what's really going on. Another's perspective can help you gain the clarity and focus you need to eliminate a limiting belief and set yourself up for success.

Protect your new beliefs by limiting contact with dream stealers. These are the Negative Ned's and Nellie's whose life purpose, it seems, is to burst your bubble! Let's face it; we're hard enough on ourselves as it is without adding other people's negative attitudes and opinions to the mix.

And finally, commit 100% to developing the knowledge and skills you need to build your believability to the point where your success is a DONE DEAL! Read your affirmations daily, dare to dream big and challenge the impossible every day!

Mick Moore, The Internet Entrepreneur™

Mick Moore "The Internet Entrepreneur," is an award-winning web designer, author, highly acclaimed internet marketing consultant, and key-note speaker. Mr. Moore is the author of the *Home Business Success Kit*, the *Ultimate Internet Business Bible* and *The Internet Entrepreneur*. He is CEO of KillerGraffix, a prominent design and marketing group, as well as CEO of Pacifica Marketing Group, Inc., both based in San Diego. What makes Mick Moore an Online Business Expert?

- Award winning Web Designer
- Leading Search Engine Optimizing Expert
- Degree in Graphic Design and Communication
- Makes his living using the same techniques featured in his books/seminars

- Co-Director and featured in the smash-hit *The Power of Mentorship - the Movie*
- Featured in *The Power of Mentorship* book series
- Featured in *Wake Up... Live the Life You Love* book series
- Featured instructor for The Learning Annex

Mick Moore dedicates his time to helping people and small business organizations understand how they can aggressively compete in today's high tech Internet market. His clients include major hotels and restaurants, government agencies, bio tech firms, lawyers and doctors. He has a proven track record delivering specialized marketing strategies for thousands of clients for over 10 years

His Seminars and Boot Camps deliver incredible insider Tips & Tricks to creating a six-figure income online. His events are fun and exciting as he takes you step by step through the process of building your own successful internet empire and sharing the secret of *Turning your PC into a Pay Check*.

Visit Mick Moore online at:
www.QuickStartExpert.com

Chapter Seven

IS A HOME BASED BUSINESS RIGHT FOR ME?
Mick Moore, The Internet Entrepreneur™

Have you been wondering whether a home based business might be right for you? Are you intrigued by the commercials you see on late night television, or the articles you read in magazines, or your former co-worker that quit, only to go on to start his own home based business? Well, you're not alone.

Home based businesses are growing at an amazing rate. In fact, some say the home based business is the wave of the future and the growth rate for home based businesses is estimated to be around 10% per year. Of course, the big question that most people want to know is: *How do I know if a home based business is right for me?*

Good question.

Several years ago, when I first started my home based business, I never dreamed I could make the kind of money I'm making today. To be honest, I didn't even intend to. At first, I just wanted a bit of extra cash to supplement my real job and, maybe, put a little money aside for the future.

But, what I discovered amazed me! Within just a few short months, my little business was raking in thousands of extra dollars every month! I was making more in a month, working part time in the evenings, than I was working 9 to 5, making profits for my boss.

As you can imagine, it wasn't long before I decided to ditch

'The Boss' and start working for myself full-time. That was back in 2000. Now, I have several business ventures that I run out of my home bringing in cash 24/7.

Each morning, I wake up, pour myself a cup of coffee and spend the next few minutes checking my emails, noting that familiar "You've Got Cash" from PayPal and making sure that my systems are working properly. The rest of the time I'm creating book covers, websites and information products for my clients and friends.

It really is that easy!

But, while the money is great, the best thing about working from home is the freedom. I'm not just making more money than I ever thought I would earn—unlike my other high-income friends… I've actually got the time to enjoy it. That's a feeling money just can't buy!

The fact is all you need to make money working from home are a few simple tools and the 'WILL' to take action and just do it. It's not about intelligence or education or who you know. It's purely about how much you're prepared to put in at the beginning to build your business and keep it running. With a little determination, you'll have everything you need to say goodbye to your day job and earn a real income for yourself, working from home.

Keep in mind that a home-based business isn't for everyone. Some people like the commute. They enjoy having a boss who tells them what to do, and they like the routine of working nine-to-five for a salary that can barely pay the mortgage. Personally, I couldn't ever do that again.

More reasonably, there are people who are concerned

about the risk of starting up their own business. They're not sure they have what it takes or that it's worth the investment of time and money, and they're terrified of the responsibility that comes with running their own company.

A home based business is not something to be taken lightly or jumped into without careful consideration.
There's a big difference between being an employee and running your own business.

1. Employees are typically told when to be at work. *Home based business owners must set their own schedules.*
2. Employees are typically told exactly what to do each day. *Home based business owners must manage their own time and prioritize their tasks.*
3. Employees can be terminated or repositioned at any time. *Home based business owners determine their own success.*

Employment, as we know it in the United States, is changing. The days of retirement and pension plans are gone. Job security is pretty much gone, as well.

Companies everywhere are downsizing. They've either gone virtual or moved offshore, eliminating jobs in all sectors. Despite this trend, the annual income for Americans has actually increased from $13 Trillion in 1991 to $40 Trillion in 2001 and is rising. So there's more than just hope. There's a whole new Business Boom happening.

Many experts attribute this boom in growth to the increase in home based businesses, primarily network marketing. In home based businesses and network marketing, opportunities come with a plethora of benefits. Many people are moving into home based businesses not only to supplement their income, but to allow for more time with family or to create a new career altogether.

Often these ventures do not require any specialized degrees or skills. Anyone can learn how to do network marketing. Just do a search on the Internet and you will find a life time of knowledge and information, and a majority of the information is free. There are business opportunities for all walks of life. Anyone can take advantage of these opportunities. There has never been a better time than the present to start one's own home based business.

One of the biggest advantages of having a home based business is the fact that one can create multiple streams of income from a wide range of services and products, thus creating an earning potential that's limitless.

You'll know it's time to consider a home based business when...

You find it hard to get out of bed and go in to the office every day. You find yourself dreading the commute, or you're just bored.

Life shouldn't be a drag, especially five days out of seven. You should be eager to start the day and the work you do should be challenging and invigorating. The ideal job or business should allow you to use skills and strengths to not just earn an income, but to contribute value and feel fulfilled. You know how great it feels to help someone out. Imagine getting paid for that, day in... day out.

Consider the type of work you would most enjoy. Can you turn that into a business that can be run from home? I'd be willing to bet the answer is a resounding... YES!

Is a Home Based Business Right For Me?
Mick Moore, The Internet Entrepreneur™

The most successful home based business begins with a great home based business idea. Successful business entrepreneurs say that you should build your home based business in your imagination before you build it in reality. What are you truly passionate about and how can you create a home based business built on that passion?

First, I suggest taking a look at what is out there already. Type in a search online about something you think you may enjoy doing and see what pops up. You'll be surprised at how many different ideas there are on the Internet that may have to do with your particular passion or skill set. Doing a little research online will help you figure out if your home based business idea can work and how you can come up with other ways to make huge money online from home.

It could be as simple as selling through online auctions such as eBay. You could sell tangible goods on the Internet, or sell a service to customers. You could also serve as a business coach or consultant to others. The opportunities are limitless.

The freedom that is available when your income is flowing from multiple streams is something that must be experienced to be believed. I wake up every morning excited to see that wonderful message from PayPal, "You've Got Cash!" My whole day starts out with the satisfaction of knowing that I made the right choice by becoming a home based business entrepreneur.

If you are looking for what you would like to do on the internet, I highly recommend that you follow something you're passionate about. Doing what you enjoy doing and getting paid for it is a great way to get through your day. Think about a favorite hobby, your area of expertise or your interests.

Begin by creating a list of ten things you enjoy doing more than anything else: maybe golfing, fishing, or just being funny. Now, create a second list, numbered 1-10, of the things at which you are most talented. This might include cooking, or bike riding, or telling jokes.

Get together with family members or friends and have them start crossing things off both lists that they feel you're not that good at until you have one "favorite" thing left and one "talent" thing left on each list.

If you find that being funny is left on the list, look back at how many of the accomplishments you had that were somehow connected to your sense of humor or making people laugh.

If you find that telling jokes was left on the talent list, look back at how many of the accomplishments you had that were somehow connected to your quick wit or your gift of gab.

The things you write on those two lists share the passion needed to achieve your goals and create a successful home based business. The more items from both lists that you bring into play, the closer you will be to finding that perfect business.

Naturally, the opposite is true. If you didn't have any of the items from your two lists involved in a goal or dream, you probably wouldn't enjoy being in a business in that particular field anyway and would most likely give up and quit long before you really got it started.

With this in mind, take a long hard look at the current list of hobbies and things you enjoy doing and see how many of them are really what you would enjoy doing for a living and how many of them would allow you to actually utilize your given skills and talents.

Do you have enough personal passion and drive behind your listed items to insure you'll go the extra mile and successfully accomplish the goals you've set for yourself and your new business? You may need to reevaluate to see if they really ignite that passion and spark that will keep you going through the exciting, challenging, and possibly difficult days ahead.

I encourage you to make several of these lists and share them with a partner, family or friends, so you can get an unbiased evaluation of your true gifts and talents. With this list in hand, there should be no doubt as to where your passions truly lie. These are the things that will help you figure out what your real passion is and allow you to create the perfect home based business.

Remember, your business idea doesn't have to be revolutionary. You can always improve on an existing idea or figure out how to market an existing product, better. This may allow you the opportunity to make a great deal of money for very little effort and have more time to enjoy your new found wealth with your friends and family.

Take the time to carefully consider what you would like your life to look like five or 10 years from now. Does your current job allow you the opportunity to make that happen? If not, then it's time to "take your future by the horns," and start your own home based business.

The bottom line is to follow your passion and do what you really enjoy doing. You'll be surprised at how doing something you love really isn't work at all and the passion and drive you have building your new business will lead to your success.

It all starts with a vision or idea and taking the necessary action to make it a reality.

Lisa Jimenez

Lisa Jimenez has helped thousands of people shatter their self-limiting beliefs and finally get the breakthrough success they were seeking. From her doctoral work in leadership at Florida Atlantic University, to her matchless experience building a business herself, to her home life as a mother of three teenagers, Lisa writes from real-world experience. Lisa's best-selling book, *Conquer Fear!* has sold over 200,000 copies and is in five languages.

Her passion is inspiring people to manifest their Big Dream and live a more abundant and prosperous life. Through personal challenge, Lisa had to learn how to move through pain, reclaim her power, and get on with creating a fantastic life for herself and her three children.

Her story will inspire you to do the same.

Don't Mess With the Princess! is a powerful message of prosperity and abundance. It is your invitation to reclaim your power, dream bigger, and create a more rich and fulfilling life. For more information on the Princess Resources and Clothing Line go to: www.ILoveThePrincess.com or www.Rx-Success.com

Lisa is the author of the best selling book, *Conquer Fear!* and several audio albums on personal development. Her Rich Life Mastermind Retreats and Coaching Programs are life-changing experiences for entrepreneurs who want to build successful businesses and live a more faith-filled and outrageous life.

She resides in Southern California and South Florida, with her three children Auriana, Beau, and Connor.

Visit Lisa Jimenez online at:
www.lisajimenez.com

Chapter Eight

BE THE SUCCESS YOU WERE CREATED TO BE
Lisa Jimenez M.Ed.

So you started your own business… Congratulations! You have just taken a step that most people only dream of. Do you really get that? Seventy five percent of the work force we interviewed said they wanted to be in business for themselves, yet less than ten percent act on that desire!

You have already proven you hold the number one ingredient for success: *Act on your true desires.*

When you act on your true desires you bring forth a power that will attract all you need to build success. You've already stepped into that power! Stop right now and notice this power working in your life. The more you are aware of this power, the greater it manifests.

I was coaching a highly successful business owner named Jeff who was trying to understand why he had no passion toward his business anymore. He had a staff of fifty people and built a successful business.

Can you guess what the problem was?

Jeff started his computer business over five years ago. Taking care of his clients IT needs lit him up! He loved his career which caused his business to grow. Jeff had to hire staff. Then more staff. And more staff. His job responsibilities altered from a behind the scenes IT guy to conducting weekly staff meetings and motivating a large work force. He stopped doing what he truly desired and started to feel burned out.

How can you keep this from happening to you?

Stay committed to your desires.

What part of building your business do you most enjoy and what part do you least enjoy? Make a list and identify these two areas. (You can put the book down and make that list NOW!) Then, powerfully choose to do the things you love about your business while delegating the rest. Just imagine waking up every morning excited about what you get to do in your business because every day you are doing what lights you up. Loving the tasks at work takes a competent team who executes the ones you least enjoy doing. You just created your perfect work scenario! And that's how you guard against burnout and help create self-motivation and momentum.

To ensure you keep that powerful momentum and continue to grow your successful business, I suggest you evaluate your mindset and how you view yourself as a business owner and successful entrepreneur.

Let's play a little game...

I want you to picture in your mind a rich person. Right now, in your mind, picture a rich person. Do you see a rich person? Describe the rich person.

Now, in your mind I want you to picture a second rich person. Do you see this rich person? Notice both of these people. Notice two rich people. Describe what you see.

And finally, I want you to picture a third rich person. Picture all three rich people in your mind. Describe what you see. What are the characteristics of these people? What do they look like? Act like? What do you notice about these three rich people?

Answer this question...

Were any of these three rich people you? Did you picture yourself as one of the rich people?

If not, why not?

Do you understand it is imperative for you to see yourself as a rich and successful person? This is important for two reasons. First, other people will see you and treat you how you see and treat yourself. Second, you will behave in the manner that you see and expect of yourself.

Success is created in the mind first.

If you believe you are smart, you will behave intelligently. If you believe you are sexy, you will behave in that way. The funny thing about this truth is it doesn't even matter if what you believe is true! Ha! Your subconscious kicks in and obeys whatever you program it to believe about yourself.

The people who create successful businesses create them because THAT IS WHO THEY ARE! Sometimes it matters little what they are selling, marketing, or promoting, the successful person becomes successful because success is what they created themselves TO BE.

What about you?

I remember the first Christmas after my divorce. The first one I would spend alone—ever. There would be no gifts to give. There would be no gifts to receive. Then one day, the postman brought a package to my front door. I tore it open and found a little blue gift box tied with a white satin ribbon. I lifted the lid to reveal a beautiful silver necklace. Who do you think sent me the gift?

The card read, "To Princess Lisa. From Princess Lisa!"

Yep! I'm the one who sent the necklace to me. While that may sound silly to you, I knew I needed to remind myself, especially during that difficult time, that I am loved. I am lovable. And everything was going to be alright.

I want you to be the biggest cheerleader for yourself in both business and your personal life. I want you to see yourself as a confident, capable, successful entrepreneur right now!

Success comes from BEING successful right now.

What habit can you create right now to help you BE a successful entrepreneur? What is your "way of being" to ensure your success? Maybe it's with follow up. You can create yourself to be phenomenal at following up with leads. You are the "Follow-Up-King!" You create a system and always return calls and emails within 24 hours. It's not even an effort for you because it is WHO YOU ARE.

Or, you could choose image: You are the diva of fashion and integrity from the inside out. When people look up the word "classy" in the dictionary, your picture is there! You always look your best and epitomize business etiquette. You are on time and treat all business colleagues and clients with respect and integrity. It's not an effort for you, for you have created yourself to BE integrity and fashion.

What about encourager? You could create yourself to be a master encourager. You are the walking, talking, faith-filled, modern-day Pollyanna. You see possibility all around you, in every situation, and with all people. This is not an effort for you at all, for you have created yourself to BE possibility and encouragement. It is who you ARE.

Do you get this? It is in the BEING that success is found. The BEING actually creates the doing.

I love entrepreneurship. I love listening to people's business ideas and encouraging them in their business plan. So I decided to take this love of entrepreneurialism and put it out in the world—not just in words, but in real actions that come from my BEING entrepreneurialism.

So, two years ago I decided that whenever I met someone who told me about a business idea, I would get their name and address and send a card with a $100 dollar check in it. The card would read, "May this small token of cash be the large token of faith I have in you and your entrepreneurial dream!"

I have done this with a bartender in Iowa who wants to be a singer, a school teacher in Florida who has a dream of being a published author, a waiter in Hawaii who told me he wants to be a professional speaker, a secretary in Paris who wants to be an ambassador and build libraries in orphanages in Southern Africa... and many, many more. The response has been amazing!

The bartender called me after receiving her check and cried, "I'm putting the $100 toward a new guitar, and I want you to know that every song I'll play with that new guitar, I'll play in your name!"

The school teacher emailed, "I'm now signing up for a

writer's course and will send you my first draft!"

The waiter in Hawaii wrote, "I'm putting the $100 toward my membership in the National Speaker's Association."

The secretary in Paris called me and said, "I made a copy of the check and posted it in my office. It reminds me that my ideas matter and my dream will make a difference!"

It has been an incredible benefit to me to BE encouragement and watch my belief and love of entrepreneurialism extend out into the world beyond words and phrases. My love of entrepreneurialism is out in the world because it is WHO I AM!

That's not the end of the story…

Last year I was speaking to a large direct sales company and told them of my commitment to entrepreneurialism. I also shared with them my big vision of a world cruise on Princess Cruise line to promote my book, *Don't Mess With the Princess!* Two weeks later, I received a card in the mail with $100 and a note that read, "Lisa, may this small token of cash be the large token of faith I have in you and your entrepreneurial dream!"

What about you?

Who do you choose to create yourself to BE? How can you reflect that in your business? Make it a part of your day and you will extend yourself into the world effortlessly and be greatly rewarded for it.

You make a difference on the planet because you chose to follow your true desire and stay committed to it. You have a profound impact on the world when you know you are created for success and you show up every day boldly willing to BE the success you were created to be!

Paul and Sarah Edwards

Paul Edwards (J.D.) and Sarah Edwards (Ph.D., LCSW) are the award-winning co-authors of *Working From Home*, the first commercially published book on the topic and sixteen other books including, *The Best Home Businesses for People 50+, The Best Home Business for the 21st Century, Changing Directions Without Losing Your Way, Cool Careers for Dummies, The Entrepreneurial Parent, Finding Your Perfect Work Getting Business to Come To You, Home-Based Business for Dummies, Home Businesses You Can Buy, Making Money with Your Computer at Home, Secrets of Self-Employment, Teaming Up: The Small Business Guide to Collaborating with Others, The Practical Dreamers Handbook, Why Aren't You Your Own Boss?* and *Making Money in Cyberspace*. Their most recent book is *Middle Class Lifeboat: Careers and Lifestyles for Navigating a Changing Economy*.

Their books, written with the purpose of helping people to do the work they want to do while living the life they want to live, have sold two million copies. They have been made into four audio titles and translated into eight languages.

Visit Paul and Sarah Edwards online at:
www.MiddleClassLifeboat.com
www.PineMountainInstitute.com
www.WishTheDoctor.com (What I wish the doctor told me).

Chapter Nine

HELP THOSE YOU MENTOR
AVOID THE PITFALLS
When Starting Their Home-Based Business
Paul and Sarah Edwards

When people first go out on their own, they're likely to be excited, optimistic... and a little apprehensive. They're asking themselves "Will I get enough customers?" "How long will it take?" "What if... ?" A bushel of mixed feelings is pretty par for the course, but consider this:

Seven in ten independent workers are satisfied with their work. That compares with just 50% of salaried employee who express a similar level of satisfaction.

To make sure the people you work with are among the satisfied, what are the pitfalls you want to help your mentees avoid? What can you do to help them avoid them?

Many people will tell them the key to success is to write a business plan, but the research is less conclusive of this as a solution. Peter Economy, the co-author of *Lessons From the Edge: Success Secrets for Starting and Growing a Business*, interviewed 75 entrepreneurs whose companies were producing over $1 million a year before the owners reached 40. According to Economy, "Almost to the person, they said they would not have done a business plan. Too often business plans are an excuse for not getting things done. They expressed the belief that it's better to dive in than to plan every move. The only time they needed a formal business plan was when they went out to get outside financing or funding."

We find this especially or even more true for most one- and two-person enterprises. We have long held that the value of a business plan for start-up businesses, which can be written in a moment of inspiration on the back of a napkin, is to stimulate one's thinking before stumbling into pitfalls, in the process wasting time, money and energy. Thus, most people benefit from writing down answers to questions like:

- Who are your most likely clients?
- What do you offer them that is distinct from what your competitors provide?
- What are the best ways for you to reach your target clients?
- What tasks do you need to do first to get underway? It's wise "to do first things first," but what is first? And what is next? And next?
- How will you price what you offer, and what do you expect your costs and revenue to be?

The answers to these questions should provide a foundation from which to launch a new venture. Our experience of more than 25 years researching, writing, and broadcasting suggests two major pitfalls to avoid as home businesses proceed. They are:

Marketing Mistakes: Year after year, survey after survey, the problem newer businesses identify is getting clients.

Money Monsters: Research by the Small Business Administration indicates money problems are the primary cause of business failure:

- Not having enough money to cover startup and operating expenses
- Not having sufficient funds with which to grow
- Insufficient funds for proper marketing
- Too much debt
- Cash-flow problems
- Inadequate financial planning
- Not charging enough to make a profit
- Poor credit and collection practices
- Inadequate bookkeeping

So let's explore what can be done to avoid these.

Mastering Marketing

For home-based businesses the lack of or ineffective marketing is a prime reason money becomes such a common pitfall. So let's consider how to avoid this first.

Based on thousands of interviews, we've concluded that the keys to building a largely self-sustaining business is word-of-mouth referrals and the best way to get this working is to tailor marketing to methods that are (1) targeted to the type of customers the small businessperson is best suited to serve, and (2) suit the individual personality of the small businesspeople so she or he will execute them willingly, if not enthusiastically. Here are some basics for doing this.

Reaching Potential Clients

Always market in fertile ground. For example, if your

mentee wants to reach clients over the age of 35, chances are blogging or podcasting won't be fertile ground because market research indicates these media are most appealing to people between the ages of 18 and 34. Instead it may be more useful to put energy effort into developing a website or networking.

Networking always rates high in the way professionals seek clients but again the key is to be sure you're networking in milieus where you'll be sure to encounter an ample number of people who need what you are offering or are in a position to refer you to others who do. Thus, to network in a chamber of commerce made up of business owners may not be an ideal place to network yourself as a career counselor, but getting involved in an industry group undergoing significant change, would.

Tailoring One's Marketing to One's Personality

Most people find they do best focusing their marketing efforts on activities they personally enjoy and do reasonably well with ease. The following are several methods that have been cited over and over when we interview people as effective ways to get businesses underway. Which ones would be appealing to you? We've grouped these under two headings: (1) Face-to-face contact and (2) The Web.

Face-to-Face Contact

- Directly soliciting individuals who are likely sources of referrals for one's business. A face-to-face call can be warmed up with an advance email, an phone call, or post cards.

- Walk Around the Neighborhood. We use neighborhood

figuratively. It means walking around locations with potential. These could be professional buildings, trade shows, conventions, and job expos. This method can be ideal for anyone who likes meeting and talking with people. Actually, this can be done any time. It doesn't involve selling. One introduces oneself, asks something about the person or business being visited and leaves a card. This marketing approach can be tucked into a schedule even on busy days by WATN (walk around the neighborhood) in the areas one's own business activities takes one to. People who do this tell us it's not unusual to get regular referrals from the locations they visit.

• Networking in business and trade organizations. Going to organizational meetings and events means connecting with potential clients and referral sources on their schedules. Within a networking organization, contacts are made, information and business intelligence traded, and business referrals are made.

There are both local and international organizations devoted solely to promoting networking among professionals. The largest of these is Business Network International,www.bni.com.

The most productive of these are business referral organizations, the essence of which can be summed up with the expression "You help me and I'll help you." Because members actively give and get business referrals, the success of the organization is measured by whether it helps its members grow their businesses. What distinguishes business referral organizations from other types of organizations where one can network is they have no overriding purpose aside from helping their members grow their businesses: i.e. they don't focus on community service or promotion of a particular profession, etc.

Online communities are also a form of networking, but most research shows people do not experience these as substitutes for face-to-face interaction. Social networking, however, on sites like Linkedin.com may lead to productive contacts.

The Web

- Have one's own website and be sure it includes keywords that are specific to one's location and specialization so that someone using a search engine looking for something in a specific area will find it.

- Take advantage of referral directories of professional organizations by posting one's profile and keeping it up-to-date. We recently were seeking coaches to interview on a professional site, for example, and found about half of the listings were out-of-date or incomplete.

- Test listing on local search services, such as Yahoo's local search service http://local.yahoo.com; Google's http://local.google.com, and Amazon's www.a9.com. Yellow page sites like Anywho www.anywho.com, and Smartpages www.superpages.com offer local listings. Approximately one out of four searches involve someone searching for something locally.

These are but a handful of many marketing methods someone can use to get out the word in launching a new business. Urge each mentee to identify two or three methods that are best suited to his or her personality and do them during whatever work hours they're not doing work for customers.

Taming the Money Monsters

Having a nest egg to help with the transition helps but may not be critical. The typical research on this question is based on the needs of companies with employees. That may not be you and probably not most of your mentees. It's not surprising for us to meet successful entrepreneurs who have started businesses with less than $100. How do they do it? Some take temp work to pay for their basic living expenses while they get their practice underway. Others continue to work a full-time job but unlock an instant stream of cash by reducing the amount withheld for taxes in anticipation of the business deductions they expect during their first year. Do urge checking with a tax professional, however, before changing one's W-4 form. If funds are needed, here are other ways people use to get underway.

- Bank loans
- Bartering
- Credit cards - zero percent rates are attractive but tricky
- Credit unions
- Disability grants
- Funds from investors, who may be relatives
- Home equity line of credit

- Inheritances
- Legal settlements
- Lending sources with specific missions, such as funds for women
- Life insurance policies, borrowing or cashing in
- Loan referral sites, such as American Express, Quicken
- Loans from relatives, friends, colleagues
- Local seed money funds.
- Retirement funds
- Savings
- SBA Loan Programs
- Selling collections or other assets
- Severance packages

Actually having a nest egg can be counterproductive if it leads to delaying marketing or unwise spending on business expenses that do not produce an income return. In cases like this, bootstrapping can lead to better decisions and a better chance of success.

Other Potential Pitfalls

There are other sources of problems to be avoided that can hinder a home business from taking off, such as:

- Insurance availability and cost, particularly health insurance
- Legal issues, such as choosing the best form of business to operate, particularly if the business

Help Those You Mentor Avoid the Pitfalls
Paul and Sarah Edwards

involves other people, licensing, and since
this is a home business, checking zoning and
condominium association regulations

- Managing time
- Tax planning and preparation
- Technology problems

Of these, one stands out. The cost and difficulty of
obtaining health insurance in the United States keeps
many Americans from striking out on their own. One
indication of this is that a higher percentage of Canadians
are self-employed than are Americans.[3] A major reason
for this is that at all Canadian residents are entitled to
public health insurance coverage. Canadians have health
insurance regardless of their type of employment.

Many self-employed individuals find that the best way to
keep their health insurance costs within reason is to get
into a group plan, such as those offered through industry
associations and professional organizations. The first task
is to find a group that offers quality health insurance at a
reasonable price. Be willing to look far and wide for the
largest groups possible. Some local chambers of commerce
arrange group plans for their members. National business
organizations also offer health insurance.

In addition, some self-employed individuals find health
insurance through their college alumni association, and
some through a union. If it's an incorporated business, or
there are employees, another possible way to get group
coverage is to lease one's employees, including the owner
from an employee leasing company. Leasing companies

can be identified by occupation or state at the website of the National Association of Professional Employer Organizations www.napeo.org.

Also, some cities, like San Diego, are forming separate legal entities to offer health insurance plans to small businesses. San Diego's plan requires a business to have at least two employees, so a husband and wife working together will qualify.

After identifying several plans, compare both the costs and benefits. Urge those you mentor to:

- Beware of "bargain" rates. They may be offered by companies with lots of complaints for nonpayment of claims or be outright scams.
- Always check with the state agency that regulates insurance to make sure that the company is registered to sell insurance in the state and second, what is the companies' record of complaints. When claims are unreasonably denied and medical bills go unpaid—as happens to too many people every year—"bargain" insurance is no bargain. The National Association of Insurance Commissioners www.naic.org is one of several websites that link to state insurance department.

If you have a health problem, like a lower spine injury or a chronic illness, one encounters even bigger problems obtaining health insurance because most groups screen individuals applying for preexisting conditions. If one can get into a plan, it's apt to have an exclusion for the condition. In this case, it may be possible to buy a separate policy covering just the risk, though this may not be affordable.

110

If one finds oneself in this situation, check to see if there's a state mandated guaranteed issuance of policies. Many states do, and some states, such as California, Colorado, Connecticut, Maryland, and Texas have specific provisions for small businesses. However, rates are apt to be higher, so it's best to talk with a health insurance broker. A broker in one's area can be found through the National Association of Health Underwriters (www.nahu.org). To find out about companies that bypass agents and sell directly to consumers, it's best to check with colleagues, or check a state insurance department's web site.

Even in a group plan, decent health insurance won't be cheap, and if one needs guaranteed coverage, it will cost between 10 and 50 percent more than regular insurance. Also there may be a waiting period before preexisting conditions are covered. If this is your situation, we advise working with a knowledgeable agent to get the best coverage you can.

An issue that comes up for many new business owners will usually work in your favor in the value of mentoring: Nine in ten small businesspeople report increasing pressure from change.

Summary

What's most important in launching and growing a home business is to be active. The key is to always move forward toward goals, and to refuse to allow obstacles—like feeling blocked by needing to do a business plan—to get in one's way.

End Notes:

1. Matthews, J.; Dennis, J.; Economy, P., Lessons From The Edge: Success Secrets for Starting and Growing a Business Oxford University Press, London, 2003, ISBN: 0195168259.
2. Edwards, P.&S., 1996, Secrets of Self-Employment, New York, NY, Tarcher/Penguin
3. Statistics Canada (http://142.206.72.67/02/02e/02e_ 007_e.htm) and US Bureau of Labor Statistics.

Casey Emerson

Casey Emerson is an author, speaker and business owner. Putting her experience and talent to work, she formed Casey Design San Diego and The Pro Writing Company. Now, as an entrepreneur, she shares her passion for inspring others to realize their potential and create their dream life.

Her current projects include writing, product development and consulting. Visit Casey online at:

www.ProWritingCo.com
www.CaseyDesignSanDiego.com
www.MyInspirationAndMotivation.com

Chapter Ten

WILL ANOTHER YEAR PASS YOU BY?
Casey Emerson

With each new year comes renewed hope for the future and reflection on the year that seemed to pass by with the blink of an eye. We promise this year will be different. We promise to make a change, accomplish our goals and finally go after what we've always wanted; only to hear ourselves say the same thing the following New Year. When does promising end and action begin?

If you find yourself in a life missing what you've always wanted, this has to be the year you finally take action. Don't wait until next week, next month or next year. The longer you wait, the longer you delay the life you've always wanted.

Of course, that's easy for me to say, right? I'm not the one reading this, you are. Actually, I am reading this. As I am writing this message for you, I am also writing it for me, just as I did one year ago.

That time seems like a lifetime ago. The need for change came more out of frustration than courage, but I had finally had enough and wanted some serious change. Stuck in the same old grind of working for someone else and not getting anywhere was getting old, and so was I—at least that's the way I felt. I was exhausted and desperate to create the life I had always wanted and it included building my own business. It had been a thought in the back of my mind for years, but every year seemed to pass me by faster than I could plan to do something about it.

Will Another Year Pass You By?
Casey Emerson

Every year I vowed that next year would be different, but it rarely was.

Changing careers can be unnerving, but the end results are worth so much more than the temporary fear. It was terrifying to start my home-based business, but knew I had to do it in order to secure my financial future. Raised with the classic blue-collar mentality of—*go to college, get a good job, work for 30 years and hope you have enough money to retire on*—kept me stuck in fear for years. That mindset never really felt right to me, but that's what I did, because it was what I thought I *had* to do.

Working for someone else was never my idea of a good time, and for me it came down to the benefits. A job was a way for me to justify what I believed my employer could provide for me that I didn't believe I could provide for myself. However, as the benefits began to disappear, the realization set in—I wasn't getting anywhere working for someone else—and I had to wake up!

It dawned on me that everything revolved around my job. Life wasn't supposed to be about cutting my personal life short five nights a week to get up the next morning and go right back to work for someone else. Life was supposed to be my choice, not what my job dictated. It also came down to value. My value was much higher than my salary at the time and if I didn't learn how to leverage it, I was going to be 70 years old and broke.

Comparing my value to my salary became such an obsession that I calculated how much time each day was devoted to my job. I started with 24 hours a day, subtracted seven hours committed to sleep and added the total time of: getting ready for work, my morning commute, total time spent on the clock (including lunch) and my afternoon commute home (accounting for traffic delays). It was at that moment I realized that 12 of my 17 available hours per day were devoted to my job. That meant that each week, I spent 60 hours dedicated to my job, while I only had 25 hours for me. That ticked me off. Obviously, I didn't expect my boss to compensate me for my personal time to and from work, but what I did expect was for my job to be worth it to me. I quickly realized it wasn't. Spending almost two hours per day in traffic was hardly building my wealth.

My mind started to fill with thoughts of what I could create with 60 additional hours per week: go back to school, have more time with my family, do the things I really love to do, start my own business... Ding! The light went on. Wow! I could finally do what I've always wanted to do—start my own business. For the first time in my life, I was about to find out just how powerful devoting 60 hours per week to my success would be.

That was it for me. I decided at that moment there were many more benefits for me and my family if I let go of living inside the boundaries that were created by my J-O-B. It was time for me to step into my potential and take control of my financial future.

Following some quick calculations, I determined that if I could increase my hourly value by 200% that would be a good start. Well, I reached that goal the minute I started my own business. My value increased by 200% overnight. I concentrated on what I was really good at and combined that with what I love to do, and started my home-based business. It was amazingly simple to create an opportunity to get paid to do exactly what I loved to do. Within a few months, it had increased my value by 300%. Boom! Instant potential. There was no going back for me.

So why had my employers gotten away with paying me only a fraction of my value? Because that's what you give away when you have a J-O-B. Your value always has to be higher than your salary. If your boss paid you a salary equal to your value, there would not be any profit margin for the company. They've been paying you $25 per hour, but your efforts earn the company $75 per hour. You get hired for your value—that's the name of the game. Whatever they pay you, they make at least double that in profits from your employment. When you cut out the J-O-B, you retain your entire value. It's like cutting out the middle man.

Strictly speaking, when it comes to owning your own home-based business, choice is unlimited. Start with what you like to do and where your expertise lies. These days, the entrepreneurial market is wide open and you have the freedom to get paid to do what you actually like to do. If you have a hobby or a talent, you can turn it into a business.

Just for a moment, think about your current job and ask yourself these questions:

- Does my job allow me to do what I like to do?
- Is my salary fulfilling my current financial needs?
- Is my job fulfilling my long-term financial goals?
- Does my family get more attention than my job?

117

If you answered *no* to any one of these questions, you have enough reason to pursue a new career—being your own boss. If your current job is not providing support of your short- and long-term goals, you owe it to yourself to create a life that will.

While some of us wish for just enough money to pay our bills, your dreams have to be much bigger. If you could create your ideal life, anything you want, what would you wish for? Would it include things like:

- More personal time
- More family time
- Increased income
- Additional income to aggressively save for retirement
- Putting your kids through college

…Or even telling your boss to take a hike!

It's OK, you can be honest—it's just you and this book right now. What do you really want? Does your current job provide the means for you to get there? If you think your employer is providing more for you than you can, think about the future of your employer-sponsored health care and retirement plans. The discouraging trend continues to show that employees will bear increased financial responsibility for their health care and retirement plans. As employers face increasing health care and money management fees, they must shift the financial responsibility to the employee in order to maintain profit margins. Let's face it, employee benefits are dwindling and that is not good news for employees.

Will Another Year Pass You By?
Casey Emerson

If you're realizing your J-O-B isn't providing the resources to take care of you—let alone your family —you're not alone. The financial resources to live the life you have always wanted will not be coming from your employer. They will only come from being your own boss.

I'm not trying to scare you, but it's important to understand what the future holds if you do not take control of your life—starting today. You only get one shot at this life, make it the kind of life you and your family deserve. You deserve to be happy and to thrive —and it's hard to thrive when you're doing the daily grind and struggling to get ahead.

Take the time to evaluate what you really want out of life and whether or not your J-O-B is providing the way to get you there. I'm not trying to tell you what to do, but I hope that by sharing my personal experience, you will be inspired to see what you CAN do. Trust me, if I can do it —you can too.

When you follow your dreams, you will change your life, change the world, and find success along the way. Life is amazing…go get some of it!

Blessings,

Casey Emerson

George Ramirez

As a successful businessman, George has started three businesses, traveled to 35 U.S. states and 26 countries. As a recognized speaker, his ability to engage an audience and truly get the message across is well known in the industry.

His affiliations and contributions include:

—Featured author in the entire *The Power of Mentorship* book series.

—Featured in the latest hit movie, *The Power of Mentorship - The Movie*

—Associate Producer and Co-Star in the movie *Pass It On*

—Member of the One Coach *Business Mastery Group*

—Contributor to the *Millionaire Mentor Team*

George focuses on training and coaching public speakers and presenters with his "Present With Purpose" boot camps producing quality results for all attendees.

Visit George Ramirez online at:
www.GeorgeRamirezAuthor.com

Chapter Eleven

WOULD YOU HIRE YOU???
George Ramirez

Welcome to the world of The Home Based Business, Entrepreneurial, Be Your Own Boss (and fire your current one!), Make Millions From Home and any other fancy title you want to give to the most demanding, challenging, frustrating endeavor you will ever undertake in your entire business life, WORKING FOR YOURSELF!!!

Now, having said all that, let me add this; it is also the most rewarding, liberating and satisfying thing you could ever do. Nothing—I mean absolutely nothing—is better than being your own boss.

Hey, think about it, would you fire you? Would you give yourself a raise? How about a longer vacation? Longer lunches? Start at 10am, lunch from 12 to 2, end your day at 4?!? Sounds almost magical, doesnt it? It does, not because it is magical but because it is a fantasy! Get this and get it good—YOU WILL HAVE TO WORK!!!

So, let's take a look at some very common sense, practical and sanity saving things you can do to make your business a success.

Make sure you really have a business; whether it is a Multi-level form or if you are the sole proprietor of an IT, plumbing, or any other kind of business.

Know your business! Too many people get excited about doing something from home and they will try anything and end up doing nothing. Become a student of your

122

business. Learn it to the point where you become an expert at it. Can you teach it to others? That is a good indicator of how well you know your stuff (besides, at that level you can be the expert and then charge for consultations/speaking, etc.)

There are NO deals when it comes to Attorneys, Legal Issues, and Taxes and, if needed, CPAs. Always hire the best you can afford. Stay away from your neighbors Uncle Jim that does taxes from his garage during tax season, while the rest of the time he is a gardener. Contracts, lease agreements, purchase orders, even your cell phone agreement is a legal contract. Never sign without an attorney reviewing it first. I know you're smart, you read English and watch court TV. Have the docs reviewed anyway or suffer later.

There are huge advantages to having a real office at home: save lots of money, write offs and more. Consult your tax person. Get the details and do it right. NO, your laundry room with your computer on the washer and printer on the dryer does not count. Besides, there is a real psychological advantage to an office that looks and serves as an office. You can actually feel like you're working. It is a truly nice feeling. Then, if you get bored and need a change of scenery, go outside. With today's WIFI systems, I do work in the front or back yard. I like that.

Get an assistant. Maybe not right away, but as quickly as financially/emotionally possible. Have them do all the things YOU DON'T LIKE TO DO, but are necessary for the success of your business. Don't be cheap. Interview or ask for referrals for someone who is like-minded and whom you can trust. Remember, they will be in your house! They will have access to just about everything in it and there may be times when you are away or at least, alone with them. Use wisdom.

Pay attention! Keep tabs on expenses, receipts and make sure anyone you hire for any service knows EXACTLY what is expected of them. You don't need the grief of having to do something over again just because it wasn't done right the first time. Hint; it may not be a good idea to have family work for you, sometimes, not even good friends. If you do, make sure that everyone understands that this is business—nothing here is personal. This can be tough to do; just think about it.

Have boundaries. Answering business calls while on a romantic dinner that you already postponed twice before, may not score many points with the wife. Can you establish set hours? How much of your business needs you in person? Or, can you do the majority of it via email, fax or regular correspondence? Either way, allow time for yourself and your family. You don't want them to resent the business.

Balance. Take time out. Take the family to the beach, mountains, mall, Disneyland. It doesn't matter, do something together. It creates deposits into their emotional bank accounts and when you really need them to understand, there will be enough on deposit to cover your withdrawal.

Stay in shape: Emotionally, Spiritually and Physically. You benefit no one dead (well, there is life insurance) but other than that, people want you around. There is no true wealth without health.

Find Mentors! Find someone who is already doing what you want to do. Just make sure that they are doing it well. This speeds up the learning curve and can eliminate many mistakes. You will learn one way or the other, by experience or wisdom. Wisdom is quicker and hurts less. I have helped start several businesses, some for myself, many for others. Stuff happens and things show up out of nowhere. It is a good idea to have your Mentors close by for counsel masterminding.

Enjoy the ride. Stay pumped up. Hang out with people that have great attitudes and will support your endeavors. Keep your eyes on the goal. This helps you to not spend too much time looking at what is going on around you that isn't helping you. Remind yourself, several times a day, about why you are doing what you are doing. You are your first and most important sale!!! Keep inspired by reading great books, listening to motivating recordings, get involved with groups that are like-minded and meet with them regularly. Remember this: Your network is truly your net-worth!

Well, here are 10 tried and true ideas that I believe will absolutely help you become and stay successful in your personal business. There are no magic bullets, secret potions nor 'get rich quick' schemes. BUT, success does leave clues and it is to your advantage to discover them and then use them.

I will end with what I know to be a Master Key to success. I am an affiliate in Bob Proctor's *Science of Getting Rich* program. W. D. Wattles states in his book that it is not enough just to do certain things, but you must do certain things in a certain way to become truly wealthy. These trainings/teachings have helped me enormously and I believe they can help you. Contact me so that I can forward you the link to this most amazing of teachings.

Now, go outside and hang your sign. After all, you are in business for YOURSELF!

Kimberly Adams

Kimberly Adams was a tax professional for over 25 years and is a testimony to the fact that it is never too late to reinvent yourself. Five years after starting her own business, Kim was able to leave traditional employment to pursue her passion of owning her own business, helping others, training and speaking. Kim has great communication skills and is a dynamic speaker. Although Kim's background is financial, it wasn't until she started her UnFranchise business with Market America that she understood the principles of achieving financial security: leverage and residual income. Kim will help you to define your passion and implement simple steps to achieving financial independence. In addition to having both her CPA and CFP® , Kim is also a Nutraceutical Consultant with nutraMetrix®, a member of both Toastmasters and the National Speakers Association, a graduate of George Ramirez's Present with Purpose training and an avid road cyclist.

Kim is happily married to Lee and is the proud mother of Elyse, her daughter, and Brian, her son.

Kim can be reached at kim@kimberlyadams.org or by calling 412-215-6115

Visit Kimberly Adams at:
www.KimberlyAdams.org
www.MarketAmerica.com/KimAdams

Chapter Twelve

YOU CAN REINVENT YOURSELF!
Kimberly Adams

Are you frustrated and stressed out? Are you making a living instead of a life? Do you have fantasies of tossing your office files into one of those large garbage bins and drafting your resignation letter? Well, this was certainly me!

You see, I had been a frustrated bean counter for quite some time. I didn't mind going to work and I liked the people with whom I worked, I just always had this yearning to have a totally fulfilling life doing what I was passionate about which was helping and mentoring others, health and fitness, success principles, public speaking AND having the time and money to hang out with my family and friends, travel, and bike more!

As a working mom, though, I had two overriding priorities, Elyse and Brian, my two wonderful children! I was fortunate that in the accounting and tax profession, I had the ability to work a reduced work schedule so I worked part-time for many years. My career was a lesser priority as I enjoyed raising my kids and I also appreciated the fact that I WAS living my dream of being married and having kids without having to work full-time. Now that I understand more about the Law of Attraction, I see that I really attracted exactly what I envisioned my life would be while raising my children — time to enjoy them growing up, a way to contribute and adult contact that the work force provided, time with my husband, Lee, and time for me! I wanted life/work balance and that is exactly what I got!

As my children got older, I became increasingly frustrated with what I was doing. I knew I wasn't really doing what I wanted to do. I have also been a personal growth and development junkie for many years. I think I first read *Think and Grow Rich* by Napoleon Hill when I was 20. I also knew that to be truly happy or financially successful, you needed to be following your passion and your bliss. I needed to start following my passions.

At this same time, my husband was going through some major health issues and I was faced with the fact that I might be the primary source of income for our family. On one hand, I was thinking "I can't do taxes for another 20 years!" But on the other hand, I was also very grateful for my well paying position and the financial security that we had created to that point so that I didn't have to return to full time work. I also had a confidence or intuition that something would change.

So, it was no surprise to me when I received a call from a neighbor who asked me if I knew anyone who was interested in starting a business part-time. I said, ME!!!! I met John on my bicycle and I would see him and his business partner, Tom, in our local coffee shop in their bike shorts a lot! I had to find out what these two were up to but I was following my intuition that something was coming my way. I'm so glad that I followed my gut. John and Tom were tremendous role models and mentors for me as I started my business and remain two of my strongest mentors and very good friends to this day.

You CAN Reinvent Yourself!
Kimberly Adams

I started my UnFranchise business with Market America in 2002 and thank God every day for it. Even as a CPA and financial planner, it wasn't until I started my business that I began to understand that to create true financial wealth, you needed to leverage your time, in addition to your money, and find a way to generate a residual income stream. I understood about leveraging your assets by investing but not how to leverage your time. I figured that if I hadn't been taught these principles, who had?

I became an avid student of the training system provided by our company which followed a franchising model. It centered not only on the specific steps to build an UnFranchise business but also on all the success principles: including attitude, goal setting and affirmations, persistence, the law of attraction and the law of association. I was already a self-improvement junkie, remember, so now I was learning great concepts on how to create wealth and my dream life but also how to help others do the same. I was in hog heaven! I have become passionate about spreading the word for what it takes to create wealth, not just in financial terms but also with respect to health and relationships. True wealth is having the time and money to do what you want, when you want and with whom you want!

One quality that has always helped me throughout my life is a positive attitude and empathy for others. I learned this from my first role models and mentors in life, my mom and dad. My mother is the epitome of faith and was always the rock of our family. My father was the compassionate, spontaneous and fun loving one and I am so grateful to both of them for all they have given me.

I am also a "reverse paranoid" as they say. I expect things to work out for my benefit and that everything that occurs in my life is for my spiritual growth. So, any time a challenge came, I would think, "What am I supposed to learn here?" I learned this from one of my mentors, Wayne Dyer. Wayne and I have never met but he is a "first name" celeb in our house. "What are you reading Mom? More Wayne?" Yes, honey, more "Wayne!"

Wayne also taught me that everything in life is a blessing even though we may not understand why at the time. This helped me get through some rough times and to always stay in an attitude of gratitude which is crucial for creating the life you want. Study the Law of Attraction to fully understand this.

Something else that I possessed that was necessary for building a business and has helped me achieve everything that I have is discipline. I have been able to set goals and accomplish them step by step. I decided to pass the CPA exam early in my career before the career's time demands set in and used self study books to do that. I had the exam passed two months into my accounting career. I went to night school to get my Masters and did it in two years by doubling up on classes.

Later, when the opportunity presented itself for me to study for the CFP certification through my firm, I jumped at the chance, studied, and passed that.

I love biking and decided that I was going to train for the MS150. This is a fundraiser for the Multiple Sclerosis Society in which you cycle 150 miles over two days. "OK, let's do it," I thought. I trained for that and have done it several times. I always have to pray for divine intervention up Cochranton Hill. This is in hilly Western Pennsylvania, by the way.

I developed a passion for public speaking which led me first to Toastmasters then, more recently, to NSA (National Speakers Association) and above all to George Ramirez's Present with Purpose Course. This interest in speaking always makes me laugh because I took a zero in Mr. Ogline's 6th grade class on my oral presentation because I wasn't getting up in front of the room! And I was a first born pleaser with great grades so I've come a long way, Baby!

I was recently listening to a CD recording of Jeff Olson's, *The Slight Edge*. This really hit home for me. The "Slight Edge" is doing the little things to be successful that are "easy to do" but "easy NOT to do." It's understanding that every little choice you make throughout your day really matters, from exercising regularly, to eating healthy, to taking one little step toward your goal or dream.

If I could help people understand one thing, it would be the compounding effect that occurs with your activities and not just your money. We all understand how interest compounds but we don't seem to apply it to our actions and understand that we also invest our time with activities that compound. One day of exercising might not matter but after 30 years of it, are you fit? Yep.

When I look back on my life, it has been about slight edge activities—exercising regularly, investing regularly, reading regularly, and now building my business regularly—one day at a time. Take action every day

133

toward your goals. Your actions compound and lead you to success in whatever you desire.

Tips to Reinvent Yourself:

1. **Build belief in yourself.** Building a business or changing course in your life takes courage and belief that you can accomplish your goals. If you don't have this, work on YOU first. Write and read positive affirmations to help program your mind and build your confidence. I heard a great comment once that has always stuck with me – "What your mind hears will eventually override what you think." This is great support for reading your affirmations out loud to yourself or put them in the voice recorder of your phone as I've done and you can listen to them whenever you get a free minute. And as my favorite bumper sticker proclaims, "Don't believe everything you think!"

2. **Become a People Magnet.** Read Dale Carnegie's, "How to Win Friends and Influence People" and implement every aspect of that book! It is a classic and time tested. Be genuinely interested in others and develop great listening skills. You will attract the type of person that you are. This is one of the principles of the Law of Attraction. Since so many businesses or any endeavor are about building relationships, this is a high priority.

3. **Define Your Passions.** What you would do even if you weren't paid. Try Janet Attwood's, *The Passion Test*.

134

4. **Set Goals and read them many times each day**. Remember, there are two types of people, those who set goals and those who work for them! Brian Tracy, another mentor whom I have not yet met, has great books on goal setting. See his *Goals* or *Eat That Frog*.

5. **Enjoy the process and the journey**. Brian Tracy also taught me that we are the happiest when we are working toward our goals than after we achieve them. You will always need to be setting higher goals for yourself.

Are you ready to reinvent yourself? All it takes is the desire and the commitment to make it happen —no matter what! Once you have this, there is no stopping you. If I can do it after more than 20 years in the rat race, you can too! Let me know if I can help you in any way. I am committed to helping you. Are YOU committed to helping you?

Don and Melinda Boyer

Don Boyer is a national speaker, has authored 3 mega selling books, and is the creator of the best selling *The Power of Mentorship* book series. With power, passion, and purpose his mission is to share with people "Who they are, what they can become, what they can do, and what they can have." Having a proven track record in coaching, Don Boyer has helped a number of companies hit the million dollar a year mark. He has been paid up to $4000.00 per employee to help them reach their selling potential and goals.

Don and Melinda are the brains behind the smash movie *The Power of Mentorship - the Movie,* conceiving, producing and starring in it.

Along with his published books, Don also has a number of best selling teaching CD's in which he address the areas of success and personal development. One of his all time best sellers is his *Professor Series* DVD's. The Professor is a wacky, colorful character Don Boyer created and plays, teaching the science behind success.

Along with her husband, Melinda is an accomplished author and speaker, as well as co-founder and CFO of their company, Real Life Teaching.

Don and Melinda are proud parents and grandparents of 9 children and 8 grandchildren.

Visit Don and Melinda Boyer online at:
www.DonBoyerAuthor.com

Chapter Thirteen

GOLDEN SERVICE
Don and Melinda Boyer

My goal is to make you feel good about saying Yes!

I make this my motto and core personal statement and have found that it has brought me the wealth, riches and good fortune of a king. Have you ever said yes to something and did not feel good about it? You said yes because it was a pain or hassle to say no. Or, have you said yes because of pressure, but inside you held resentment and anger? Sure you have; we all have and it does not feel good. Like the little boy told his dad, "I will sit down, but I am standing up on the inside!"

There is nothing worse than saying yes when you really want to say no. But on the other side of the coin, there is nothing better than feeling good about saying Yes. I have bought things from salesman not because I really wanted them and certainly not because I needed them, but because the salesperson had a fantastic way of making me feel great about having those things.

Feeling good is something that every normal human being wants, desires and even craves. We will exchange our money, time and energy for it. We follow people, ideas, movements, trends, churches and groups that make us feel good. What a difference it is to go to a restaurant where the waiter is in a good mood and has an attitude of service instead of a restaurant where the waiter just has an *Attitude.* One makes you feel good about paying the bill; the other makes you resentful about paying the bill.

138

If you want to become rich and want to enjoy that wealth, you must learn the skill and take on the commitment that you will do your best to help everyone in your life...

"Feel Good About Saying Yes"

This is giving people "Golden Service," and it starts first from a mindset and then is followed by your actions. If you try to adopt the method of making people feel good by your actions only, you will fall into the category of being a "Salesman that is full of bull." That is being a con-artist who is only interested in money and is willing to tell people anything in order to get a sale. That is not the road to making people feel good about saying Yes. That is the road to having your teeth knocked out by a disgruntled customer.

You must first have the mindset that your desire is to see good come upon all those whom you serve, whether that is your customer, client, family, friend, or employer. With that mindset, you will never push or try to "sell" anything to anyone if it was not in their best interest. Your goal is find out what people want and then provide it to them with more product value than the cash value you take from them.

Take this book, for example. The ink and paper may not be worth the price you paid for it, but if the information gives you ideas and concepts that can drastically improve your life and finances, then I gave you more product value than the cash value I took from you. My goal in writing this book is to make you *feel good about saying Yes* to buying this book, and I knew the only way that could happen was if the information in this book improved your life. That way we both win; it is the ultimate win-win combination.

When you have the mental mindset of this kind of golden service, even when your request may be difficult for the other person, they will still feel good about saying yes to your request because doing so is in their best interest. As a public speaker, having a million dollar smile is very important to me (as well as those I speak to, I am sure!) so when it was time for me to have some major cosmetic dental work done, I was not doing cartwheels about it.

When my dentist told me that I needed to go through three major oral surgeries that included bone replacement, multi-procedures over a year and half time period and the cost would be thirty thousand dollars; do you think I was happy about that? However, because having a great smile was so important to me, *I felt good about saying Yes.*

In fact, my ability for feeling good about saying Yes was what gave me the strength to endure the intense procedures and healing process. Now, every morning and night when I brush my teeth or when I speak to people, I get to feel that great feeling of saying Yes all over again. Although that dental work was difficult to go through, it felt good to say Yes because I knew it was in my best interest.

You cannot make someone feel good about saying Yes if your request is not in their best interest. If the only reason you want someone to say yes to what you are offering them is because of what you will gain and profit from it, that person should say no and then proceed to kick your Butt. I know I would...and I would feel good about it, too!

I have clients worldwide who invest thousands of

dollars in my products and services because they know everything I bring them is always in their best interest and that they get more product value than the cash value they give me. My clients, customers and partners know that I am dedicated to their success. If my product does not make a person feel good about saying Yes to it, I do not sell it to them because I know that it is not a right fit for them at this time.

If I catch the slightest hesitation that someone will not feel good about saying Yes to what I am offering, I will do everything in my power to talk them out of buying it. If they have doubts, I flat out refuse to do business with them. Many people have thought that I use this method as reverse psychology in selling, but I don't. I know that there are millions of people out there who believe my services and products are an answer to their prayers. I do not need or want to do business with people if my service is not a blessing to them.

The same goes for you. No matter what you sell or do in the way of service, somebody needs you...and those people will feel good about saying Yes to what you are offering.

Create the goal and mindset that people will feel great, fantastic and wonderful about doing business with you and saying Yes to your products and services. That can only come when you understand the great law of attraction and realize that your wealth does not come from people but from the power of your thoughts.

When you understand that your gold is in your mind and

not in trying to get into people's pockets, you will find people giving you what is in their pockets in exchange for what's in your mind. Get a grip on that truth and you will find no problem in making your life center on providing Golden Service to people. When giving this kind of service to people you will always find that…

People will feel good about saying Yes!

Bonus Chapter

THE SCIENCE OF GETTING RICH
By Don Boyer

If you asked the average person what is the secret to getting Rich, many would say, "You must go in early and stay late, so that someday you can go in late and leave early." In other words — Hard Work.

Unfortunately, that is a demented plan that rarely works. Some of the hardest working people I know struggle from pay check to pay check, and some of the richest people I know are always on an exotic vacation!

Right now, millions of people are living in their dream home, driving their dream car, married to their ideal mate and living the life of their dreams. Isn't it your turn to start living your dreams?

When my mentor posed that question to me many years ago I thought in my mind, "Hell, yes, it's time!" But there was just one problem: I did not know what my next step was to get there. I did not how to do it.

In those days, my life was completely upside down; I was financially broke—ok, financially challenged—driving a broken down old car and had nothing to show in the way of material success. I stayed in that condition until I learned the Secret, the secret of the Science of Getting Rich.

You see, there is a hard way and an easy way to life. The question is, "Which way will you choose?" 97% of people choose the hard way, not because they want to but because they are not aware of the easy way. My mentor, Bob Proctor, told me at breakfast one day, "People do not earn $100,000.00 a year because they want to; they earn $100,000.00 a year because they do not have the awareness to earn that much in a month."

The Hard Way

The hard way, which I used myself for many years, is to work hard, save every penny you can, fight your way to the top, sacrifice, and never give up. Well, that is a fine plan to build an ulcer in your stomach, but not the plan to get rich. This is trying to create success from without. The secret to all success and all wealth is to learn to live your life from within, which is…

The Easy Way

Struggle, sacrifice and hard times are not necessary to become rich, but in fact, will cause riches to flee from you. The truth of the matter is, you can be, do and have anything you desire and have it all come to you without pain struggle or distress.

I know this may sound crazy to you and be something that you may have a hard time conceiving, let alone believing. However, I assure you it is all true. The best news is, we can teach you how to do this.

Let me ask you a question, "Is the plan of hard work, sacrifice, scrimping and saving bringing you the riches and success you want? If the answer is no, then my friend, you need a new plan.

Working hard on things that don't work, doesn't make them work!

If you want to change things around in every aspect of your life, if you truly want to become financially rich…the easy way, then you must learn The Science of Getting Rich. And, in order for you to learn this system it will require 3 things:

1. You must be willing to invest in yourself. If you do not invest in yourself you cannot possibly think that anyone else will invest in you.

2. Time; it will require you to take some time out of your busy day to invest in learning this easy to understand system.

3. You must take action. Stop making excuses why you cannot take action and just do it.

If you are sick and tired of being sick and tired of not reaching your dreams, and you want to really become financially Rich then go to my personal website at www.ThePowerOfMentorship.theSGRprogram.com and see how you can now learn The Science of Getting Rich for yourself.

You are only a click away from learning the Secret of having all the money and freedom you could possibly desire. Do you want to live the hard way and never get what you really desire, or the easy way and get everything you want? The Choice is yours…choose well, my friend!

www.ThePowerOfMentorship.theSGRprogram.com

FIND A MENTOR

Master Mentor Biographies

The Following Pages
Contain a List of
Mentors Who Have
Contributed to Other
The Power of Mentorship
Books.

All of Them Are
Prepared to Help You
Become The Best
You Can Be.

DC CORDOVA

 DC is the CEO of the organization that has presented the world-famous Money & You® Program, the Excellerated Business Schools® for Entrepreneurs and other Excellerated programs since 1979. She continued with the work after the creators of the programs went on to develop other breakthrough technologies. She has had the honor of working and studying with some of the best business educators and entrepreneurs in the world, and has been involved in business and entrepreneurial education for nearly three decades. She is considered to be one of the pioneers of "New Education"—high-speed entrepreneurial business education.

She is considered a "Mentor of Nurturing" and works closely with top management teams and businesses to empower good relationships. She is an author of the comprehensive systems manual for entrepreneurs, *Money-Making Systems for People who Work with People; The Power of Mentorship: The Millionaire Within* book series; and is currently writing *The Money & You® Book*. She has been a celebrity guest on several television shows and a guest speaker on many radio shows around the world.

She is an Ambassador of New Education and travels the world speaking with top business people, dignitaries, politicians, and persons of high influence. Her focus is promoting the transformation of educational systems so young people can then learn to handle money business and life from an early age and ensure their success as adults.

Visit DC Cordova online at:

www.excellerated.com

DR. JOHN DEMARTINI

Dr. John Demartini is a world leading inspirational speaker and author at the forefront of the burgeoning personal and professional development industry. His scope of knowledge and experience is a culmination of 34 years of research and studies of more than 28,000 texts into over 200 different disciplines ranging from psychology, philosophy, metaphysics, theology, neurology and physiology.

Born in Houston, Texas, Dr. Demartini is one of two children. At the age of seven he was told he had a learning disability and would never read, write or communicate. At 14, he was a high school drop-out living on the streets and panhandling for food to survive. After a near death experience at 17, due to severe strychnine poisoning, Dr. Demartini made a decision that would change his life forever.

Dr. Demartini has captured the attention of celebrities, international sport personalities, noted politicians and UN representatives as the result of a self help methodology he developed and coined as 'The Demartini Method'®. Derived from a study of Quantum Physics.

'The Demartini Method'® is now being studied in a number of Universities and presented to psychologists, psychiatrists, social workers, health professionals and prison workers all over the world.

Visit Dr. Demartini online at:

www.DrDemartini.com

MARIE DIAMOND

 Marie Diamond is an internationally known Feng Shui Master and has been practicing for more than 20 years, refining the knowledge given to her at an early age.

Born in Belgium, she was trained as a lawyer and criminologist and worked for the Belgian and European governments and then as a project manager for a multinational publishing company. She has training and experience in all forms of management including Human Resources, Marketing, Safety, and Sales.

She is part of the Transformational Leadership Council created by Jack Canfield, which includes such respected members as Bill Harris, John Gray, John Assaraf, DC Cordova, Paul Scheele, and many others.

She has been featured in several TV and Film projects including *The Secret* (2006), *I Married A Princess* (2005), and *The Jerry Hall Heaven and Earth Show* (2005).

Visit Marie Diamond online at:

www.MarieDiamond.com

PAUL MARTINELLI

As Bob Proctor's teaching and business partner, Paul Martinelli shares the international stage and collaborates with Bob to teach people how to achieve their dreams. Paul is a dynamic entrepreneur and President of Life Success Consulting.

Before teaming up with Bob Proctor, Paul worked with Guardian Angels to bring safety and education to some of the most challenging neighborhoods in the United States.

Paul is a recipient of Northwood University's Entrepreneur of the Year award and has gained an international reputation as a public speaker and leader in the personal development industry.

Visit Paul Martinelli online at:

www.LifeSuccessConsultants.com

PAULETTE BETHEL

 Paulette Bethel is a published author, editor, public speaker and web designer. As a student of Metaphysics, Paulette has owned a bookstore, facilitated *A Course in Miracles*, had a successful counseling/ Rebirthing practice, and edited the metaphysical newspaper, *Insights*.

She has hosted a two-hour talk radio show about animals and, as a long time animal lover, she co-founded a non-profit animal therapy organization for which she was Training Director for 10 years. The book, *The Good Shepherd*, by Jo Coudert highlights the innovative therapeutic techniques Paulette helped develop.

Visit Paulette Bethel online at:

www.ProEditingService.com
www.Dobermans.net
www.HowToChooseAPuppy.com

ROBIN JAY

 Robin Jay worked as an Advertising Account manager more than 18 years. She experienced a 2000% increase in sales in her career, largely because of her ability to build strong, long-lasting relationships. During that time, Robin personally hosted more than 3,000 client lunches making her the undisputed 'Queen of the Business Lunch!'

Now, as a professional keynote speaker, award-winning author and corporate trainer, Robin is not just the 'Queen of the Business Lunch,' but is a business relationship expert who shares the nuts-and-bolts of building profitable business relationships.

Jay's proven ability to communicate the laws of the universe in language that everyone can understand, to deliver messages that motivate and inspire her audiences in accordance with those laws, transforms her audiences through a journey of increased self-actualization and greater success, both personally and professionally.

Jay's books include: *The Art of the Business Lunch – Building Relationships Between 12 and 2* (Career Press, 2006). This award-winning book has been sold in ten languages worldwide, and is also available in Audio formats. Other books include *The POWER of Mentorship - The Millionaire Within, The Power of Mentorship For the Woman Entrepreneur* and *Chicken Soup for the Wine Lover's Soul.*

Visit Robin Jay online at:

www.RobinJay.com

SHELLEY KIMBERLY

Shelley Kimberly has an identical twin sister, a successful chiropractor; and an older brother, the Vice President of a local insurance company. She is the wife of a very supportive and successful dentist, a mother of three fun-loving kids, nicknamed Mak, KeKe, and RyRy. She also has two very committed and supportive parents who are a big part of her life. She has come to realize that her experiences and relationships with others has changed her life in a profound way.

Shelley has been involved in the health and wellness aspect of network marketing since 1998. Her studies in college have given her the skills needed to become a successful business woman. She has a BS in Education with a concentration in Accounting. Shelley is the president of an investment club she formed in 1998 and a member of a 'Mastermind Group.' She is also a Marketing Executive for Freelife International.

I have learned that personal growth comes from enriching others lives. I do this by promoting a healthy lifestyle, teaching the power of leverage, residual income, and showing others that working from home gives a person flexibility, freedom, and financial gain to be accountable to one self. Sharing this method has been very empowering and gratifying. To be able to affect change in people's lives in a positive way has helped motivate me to be compassionate towards others. As a mentor I have watched them "break out" of their comfort zones and gain confidence through their fulfilled dreams.

One of my mentors, my very dear grandmother, Mania, taught me it is a greater gift to give than to receive. I hope to leave that legacy for my children.

I can only imagine how your life will change by finding a mentor to help you balance your life, overcoming your adversities so that you can turn your dreams into reality. I tell others, never let the little kid in you get lost—when you were a child the tooth fairy was a "reality" and waking up the morning after losing a tooth brought such joy because of the belief you had —find what you are compassionate about and believe you can make it happen.

Whether your mentor is a family member, friend, business partner or someone you connected to in this book, find someone you can lean on that will not shatter your dreams. Believe in yourself and your desires will become your reality!

To connect with Shelley for mentoring, to find out more about becoming a business partner in Freelife, or to receive information about Freelife's product line contact Shelley via email at shelleyk@raex.com or cyberhealth@FreeLife. com or by phone (330)472-4211.

Visit Shelley Kimberly online at:

www.cyberhealth.freelife.com
www.gojipress.com
www.momslemonadestand.com

Vic Johnson

Vic Johnson is a Ponte Vedra Beach, Florida-based Internet infopreneur, author, motivational speaker and founder of a host of personal development websites.

Formerly the founder of a corporate and political communications firm, he has provided strategic consulting and planning to Governors, Members of Congress, Fortune 500 companies and non-profit organizations. His non-traditional strategies have been highlighted by major news outlets like the *Miami Herald, Washington Post* and national trade publications.

Vic bought his first business at the age of 23 and several years later became one of the early pioneers of the 'quick-lube' business, building the first locations in Florida.

His latest ventures have been Internet-based where he has quickly demonstrated his entrepreneurial acumen. Talk show host Mike Litman called one of his sites, AsAManThinketh.net, "the hottest personal development site on the Internet today." Subscribers hail from more than 90 countries and have downloaded over 300,000 eBook copies of James Allen's classic. His other websites are found at MyDailyInsights.com, mp3Motivators.com, Goals-2-Go.com and VicJohnson.com.

Visit Vic Johnson online at:

www.VicJohnson.com

158

DR. TONY ALESSANDRA

Dr. Tony Alessandra helps companies build customers, relationships, and the bottom-line. Companies learn how to achieve market dominance through specific strategies designed to outmarket, outsell, and outservice the competition.

Dr. Alessandra has a street-wise, college-smart perspective on business, having fought his way out of NYC to eventually realizing success as a graduate professor of marketing, entrepreneur, business author, and keynote speaker. He earned his MBA from the University of Connecticut – and his PhD in marketing from Georgia State University.

Dr. Alessandra is president of Online Assessments (www. OnlineAC.com), a company that offers online assessments and tests; co-founder of www.mentorU.com, an online e-learning company; and Chairman of the Board of BrainX, a company that offers online digital accelerated-learning programs.

Dr. Alessandra is a widely published author with 14 books translated into 17 foreign languages.

Visit Tony Alessandra online at:

www.alessandra.com

The Power of Mentorship For The Home Based Business
Don Boyer

Quick Order Form
The POWER of Mentorship
For the Home Based Business
By Don and Melinda Boyer
$19.95

Shipping: $2.50 for first book
$1.25 for each additional book
(California residents add 8.25% sales tax)

Fax Orders Send this form to: 562-945-5457	**Telephone Orders** Call Toll Free: 1-866-871-4487 (Have your credit card ready)
E-mail Orders melindatavera@realifeteaching.com	

Name _____

Address: _____

City/State/Zip: _____

Phone: _____

Email: _____

Method of Payment: Visa _____ or Master Card _____

Card Number: _____

Name on Card: _____

Expiration Date: _____

3-digit security code on back of card: _____

(If billing address is different from shipping address, please provide.)

The Power of Mentorship For The Home Based Business
Don Boyer

10 EVALUATION POINTS TO DETERMINE IF BECOMING A CO-AUTHOR IN ONE OF OUR POWER OF MENTORSHIP BOOKS IS RIGHT FOR YOU

Let me start of by telling you a true story. My mind races back to the early 70's when I was just a child and loved to watch *The Waltons* on T.V. Perhaps my favorite character was John-Boy because I identified with him about wanting to be a writer.

Since the age of 12, I knew that I wanted to write. When I read an ad in a comic book, How to Become a Writer, I rustled some money from my folks and sent for the home course.

I can still remember the day I got the package in the mail; my heart raced with excitement and my mind zoomed with adventure. It was a brown, soft-bound book and when I started to read it, I remember thinking, "I don't have a clue what this book is saying." But it didn't matter to me; just having that book gave me hope and inspiration!

I share this story with you because there are many reasons why someone wants to write a book. However this is what I have found out. Millions of people want to write a book. Most have the ability, some have the drive but few have the know how.

Here is my promise to you. After you evaluate these 10 points, you will know — without a shadow of a doubt — if this project is for you.

That being said, here are 10 points to evaluate to see if becoming a Co-Author in our Power of Mentorship book series is right for you:

1. **Celebrity Status**. Let's face it; we live in a society that is obsessed with celebrities. People willingly spend their money on anyone or anything they deem to be a celebrity. This is why celebrity endorsements are so important in selling products. When you become a Co-Author in one of our books, you get instant Celebrity Status. People look and treat you differently (better).

2. **Massive Exposure**. As of today, we have eight *Power of Mentorship* books out and 27,000 copies in the marketplace with sales in the US, UK, Canada, New Zealand, and Australia. These books are in the hands of a target market, the niche market that wants to buy what you are selling! If your story, name, business, website and contact information were in front of 27,000 people who are in your target market, do you think that could increase your business? Here is what I want you to do. Go to Google or MSN or any search engine and type in *Power of Mentorship*, and you will see we are all over the place. This is massive exposure.

3. **Power of Association.** Perhaps the masses have not heard of you or me, but they know national speakers, writers, and film stars like Jim Rohn, Brian Tracy, Zig Ziglar, Bob Proctor and Denis Waitley. When people see you co-authoring a book

with these celebrities, they associate you with them.

4. **Credibility**. Once you become a published author, you become an expert in the minds of people. Now you combine this with the power of association with celebrities and your creditability is instantly established. Who would not want to do business with you?

5. **Business Card on Steroids.** People throw away business cards and brochures, no matter how fancy they are. But they will not throw away a book! They will keep that book, read it and re-read it. Your information is right there in front of them all the time. Talk about a business card with power!

6. **The Power of First Impression**. How many of your competitors are sending their prospects a book that they co-authored with nationally known mentors? Talk about impressing your future clients; you won't just blow their socks off, you will blow their darn shorts off, too.

7. **Easy to get published.** We make this process so easy a child could do it. There are three ways to do this. You write your story and we professionally put it into chapter form, or we do a phone interview with you and turn that into your chapter, or we will ghost write the entire chapter for you. How easy is that?

8. **Profit Center**. Now you have a product you own that will earn you a 55% profit. Our books are of the highest quality and the content is so good they are a stand alone product. What this means is someone would buy this book in a bookstore or on the internet because of its quality. Some of our authors have sold over 500 books in a single month. You make a $13.23 profit on every book you sell.

9. **Increased Business.** We had one author land a $10,000 speaking gig because an event planner read her chapter and was so impressed she was booked for a major event. Another author got an $8,000.00 consulting job because of someone reading his chapter. The list of increased business many of our co-authors have experienced has been incredible.

10. **We pay all the publishing costs.** As a publisher, we pay for all the professional editing, formatting, book cover design, marketing campaigns and printing of the books. The only requirement you have as a coauthor is to purchase 500 books at the discount price of $6.72 per book. The book retails for $19.95, and your profit is $13.23 per book. We also supply you with a professional press release and sales aids to help you market and sell your books. This is a team venture.

Let me ask you, "Do you believe that massive exposure to a targeted market and leveraging yourself in a position that your competitors cannot touch could help explode your business, income and profits?"

If you answered yes, than being a co-author in *The Power of Mentorship* Book Series is right for you. Top this off with the fact that this type of dynamic marketing does not cost you, but pays you from the profits you get selling some of your books... it just does not get any better than this.

Please view all *The Power of Mentorship* books at www. amazon.com or go to www.DonBoyerAuthor.com.

Well, there you go; honest, open facts for you to consider. Whatever you do, we are here to help and support all your dreams and goals. Until we hear from you, we wish you the best of success.

Our Best,
Don and Melinda Boyer/Mel Brodsky
Real Life Teaching, Inc.
www.DonBoyerAuthor.com

Call us today at 562-789-1909 and see if there are any spots still available in our upcoming book. In a matter of weeks, you could be the featured co-author in the next *Power of Mentorship* Book. Call us right now!